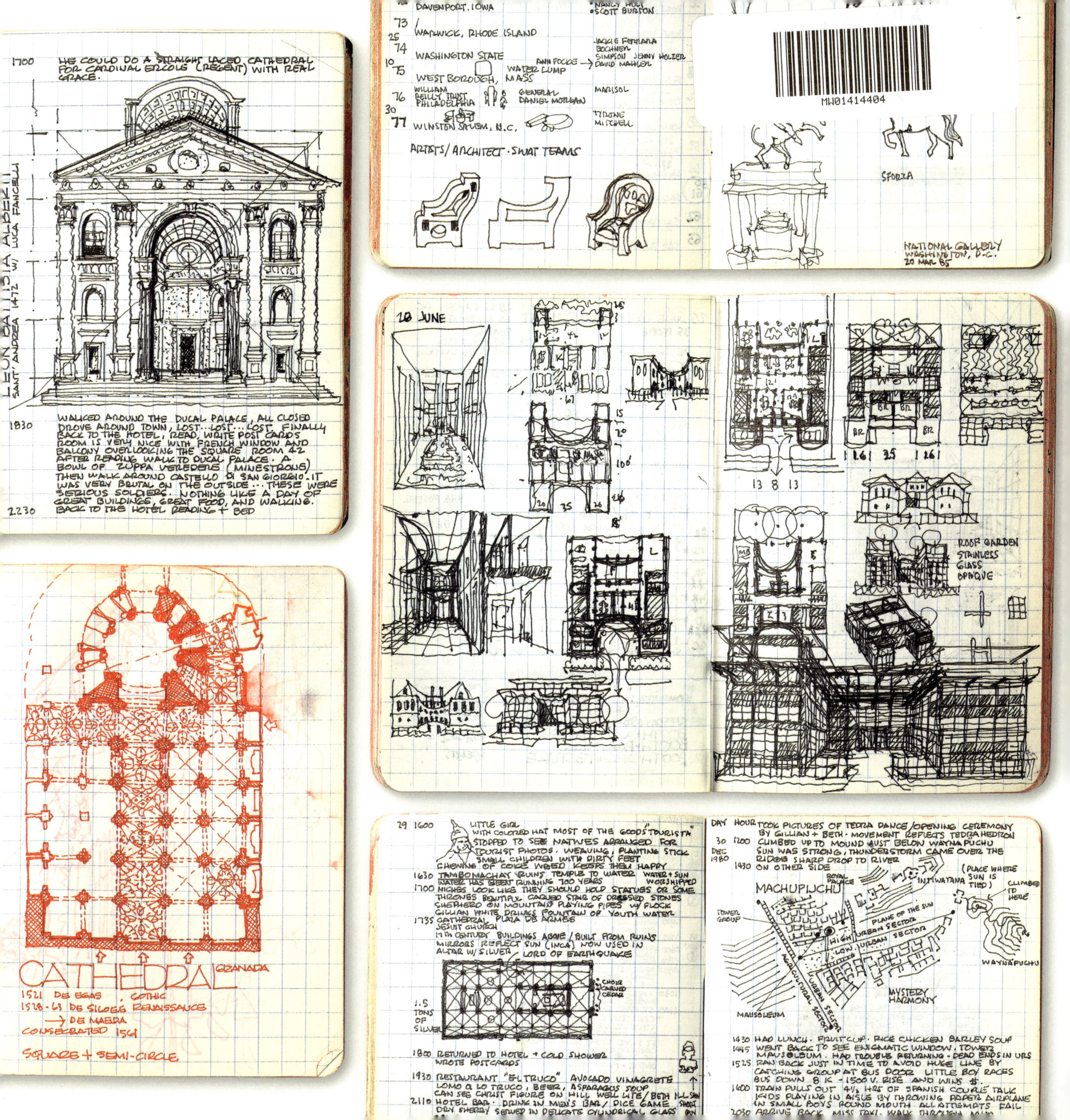

DAVENPORT, IOWA
WARWICK, RHODE ISLAND
WASHINGTON STATE
WEST BOROUGH, MASS
WATER LUMP
WILLIAM PENN TRUST PHILADELPHIA
GENERAL DANIEL MORGAN
WINSTON SALEM, N.C.
SCOTT BURTON
JACKIE FERRARA
SIMPSON
JENNY HOLZER
DAVID MAHLER
MARISOL
TYRONE MITCHELL
ARTISTS/ARCHITECT · SWAT TEAMS
SFORZA
NATIONAL GALLERY WASHINGTON, D.C. 20 MAR 85
HE COULD DO A STRAIGHT LACED CATHEDRAL FOR CARDINAL ERCOLE (REGENT) WITH REAL GRACE.
LEON BATTISTA ALBERTI
SANT' ANDREA 1472 W/ LUCA FANCELLI
WALKED AROUND THE DUCAL PALACE, ALL CLOSED DROVE AROUND TOWN, LOST... LOST... LOST. FINALLY BACK TO THE HOTEL, READ, WRITE POST CARDS ROOM IS VERY NICE WITH FRENCH WINDOW AND BALCONY OVERLOOKING THE SQUARE. ROOM 42 AFTER READING WALK TO DUCAL PALACE. A BOWL OF ZUPPA VERDERE (MINESTRONE) THEN WALK AROUND CASTELLO DI SAN GIORGIO. IT WAS VERY BRUTAL ON THE OUTSIDE... THESE WERE SERIOUS SOLDIERS. NOTHING LIKE A DAY OF GREAT BUILDINGS, GREAT FOOD, AND WALKING. BACK TO THE HOTEL READING + BED
20 JUNE
ROOF GARDEN
STAINLESS
GLASS
OPAQUE
CATHEDRAL
GRANADA
1521 DE EGAS GOTHIC
1528-63 DE SILOEE RENAISSANCE
→ DE MAEDA
CONSECRATED 1561
SQUARE + SEMI-CIRCLE
LITTLE GIRL WITH COLORED HAT MOST OF THE GOODS "TOURISTA"
STOPPED TO SEE NATIVES ARRANGED FOR TOURIST PHOTOS. WEAVING, PLANTING STICK SMALL CHILDREN WITH DIRTY FEET
TAMBOMACHAY RUINS TEMPLE TO WATER
WATER HAS BEEN RUNNING 700 YEARS
NICHES LOOK LIKE THEY SHOULD HOLD STATUES OR SOME THRONES
CATHEDRAL PLAZA DE ARMAS
JESUIT CHURCH
17TH CENTURY BUILDINGS ABOVE / BUILT FROM RUINS
1.5 TONS OF SILVER
RETURNED TO HOTEL + COLD SHOWER
WROTE POST CARDS
RESTAURANT "EL TRUCO" AVOCADO VINAGRETE
HOTEL BAR
TOOK PICTURES OF TEDRA DANCE / OPENING CEREMONY BY GILLIAN + BETH · MOVEMENT REFLECTS TETRAHEDRON
CLIMBED UP TO MOUND JUST BELOW WAYNAPUCHU
SUN WAS STRONG, THUNDERSTORM CAME OVER THE RIDGE SHARP DROP TO RIVER ON OTHER SIDE
MACHUPICHU
INTIWATANA
ROYAL PALACE
TOWER GROUP
HIGH URBAN SECTOR
LOW URBAN SECTOR
AGRICULTURAL SECTOR
PLANE OF THE SUN
WAYNAPUCHU
MYSTERY HARMONY
MAUSOLEUM
HAD LUNCH · FRUITCUP · RICE CHICKEN BARLEY SOUP
WENT BACK TO SEE ENIGMATIC WINDOW, TOWER MAUSOLEUM.

Modern Beyond Style
and the Pursuit of Beauty

To beautiful places that people treasure.

**Booth Hansen and the
Architecture of Laurence Booth**

Modern Beyond Style
and the Pursuit of Beauty

Jay Pridmore

Contents

Acknowledgements 7

Foreword 9
"Architects have been achieving their objectives with a rich language that continues to evolve. The poetry of architecture emerges when it is used in inspired and beautiful ways." *Laurence Booth*

Introduction 11
The architecture of Larry Booth and Booth Hansen achieves creative results through adherence to a reliable process. As ideas are distilled, refined and iterated, the elements of any project can be blended into a design that is both functional and beautiful, every time, never twice the same.

Beginnings 13
As a young man, Laurence "Larry" Booth was motivated by the creative potential of architecture and its ability to achieve a wide range of objectives. It set him on a career to blend form with function, innovation with tradition, and the practical with artistic elements of the built environment.

System 19
Larry viewed architecture as an effort to bring order to complex requirements. His early-career interest in sculpture represented experiments in geometric patterns. His buildings were designed as the manipulation of basic shapes to create unique form and satisfy multiple functions.

Kemper Hall
ARCO Service Station
Barglow House
The Atrium
Barr House
Magnuson House
Fox House
Museum of Contemporary Art

Process 39
Larry devised his process with a step-by-step understanding of objectives for any commission and the assembling of elements to meet them. A disciplined approach to render those elements in an optimal form for its function led to designs without minimalist or traditionalist preconceptions, rather an architecture that Larry would term "modern beyond style."

Adamson House
House of Light
Chicken Coop and Zinc House
Grace Place Episcopal
Navy Pier
Kinkead Pavilion

Spirit *67*

By mid-career Larry had learned that spirit in architecture was an attainable goal. It was achieved through memory, wrought of traditional elements too rarely found in mid-century modernism. Larry believed that richness of a building's spirit would depend upon the layering of aesthetic gestures handed down by history.

Shoreacres
Dunes Club
Schuler House
Motorola Museum of Electronics
Benninghoven House
Old St. Patrick's Church
Cleveland Court
Cline House
Ganz Hall
The Chicken Factory
Coyne Vocational College
MacLean Museum of Asian Art

Total Performance *113*

As the demands of architecture increase in complexity, design teams include engineers, consultants and other specialists. To guide collaboration, Booth Hansen uses "Compass Points" to assure that the design process is driven by common values of all involved.

Republic Windows and Doors
School of the Art Institute of Chicago
Kohl Museum
Joffrey Tower
SoNo Tower
Cook County Circuit Court
Bucksbaum House
30 West Oak Street
Palmolive Residences
The Parker Fulton Market

Beauty *155*

Beauty is architecture's sublime reward. It lies in the deep harmonies that buildings reveal in form, function and spirit. Philosophers called beauty the "splendor of truth." Booth Hansen seeks to create architecture that appears to be as inevitable a solution to its purpose as nature itself.

Chicago Botanic Garden
Mohawk Street Residence
New Buffalo Residence
Deming Place Condominiums
Palm 2150

Permanence *179*

Across the decades Booth Hansen has changed along with new conditions and changing needs. From the beginning, Larry Booth's architecture has remained fresh and up-to-date, driven not by style but by values, touched by tradition and indispensable to the future.

Kohl-Feinerman House
Glassberg House
Usher House
61 East Banks Street
Daxton Hotel
St. Joseph Island Residence

A Chicago Seven Press book.

Co-published by Steel Bridge Editions.

Chicago Seven Books is a publisher dedicated to topics of Chicago architecture.

Steel Bridge Editions is a publisher and producer of books on architecture, history and biography.

© 2023 Booth Hansen

ISBN: 979-8-218-03731-4

First Edition
Library of Congress Control Number: 2022913281

Book design by Alessandro Franchini, Chicago

Printed by the Graphic Arts Studio Inc., Barrington, Illinois

Endpapers: Laurence Booth sketchbooks; photography by Alan Shortall, Chicago

Frontispiece: Holy water font in the restored Old St. Patrick's Church. Chicago, 1997

Illustration opposite Introduction: Painting by Scott Urness

VII CHICAGO 7 PRESS

Acknowledgements

Many people on the Booth Hansen team were helpful in interpreting the principles and practice of architecture at the firm. These are dependent in so many ways on teamwork. Among those people are Scott Cyphers, David Mann, Chris Guido, Karen Fippinger and Caroline Slota. Also indispensable was artist and consultant Giselle Taxil who explained in loving detail the technique used in the creation of ornament at Old St. Patrick's Church.

As clients and people close to them are also essential members of the design team, interviews with those individuals were enlightening in understanding the process in general and their projects in particular. Those clients include Barry MacLean, Richard Pegg, Diane Lipman, Father Jack Wall, Deanna Fox, Richard Cline, Jack Schuler and Paul and Susan Zucker.

Production of a book of this sort involves many people. Alessandro Franchini was the graphic designer whose high standards are evident on every page. Editor and proofreader June Sawyers applied her customary skill to the text. The printer, Graphic Arts Studio Inc., made the book an elegant work.

As the photo credits show, many photographers were involved in the visual content of *Modern Beyond Style*. Michelle Litvin was particularly important in interpreting the work of Booth Hansen for this book.

Larry's family was involved and helpful in many steps along the way. Pat Booth and Victoria Booth read the many versions of the manuscript and made it better each time they did so. Most of all, the author is grateful to Larry Booth, whose patience in the process of imagining and creating a book, was clearly drawn from his experience in the even more exacting process of creating architecture.

Jay Pridmore
January 2023

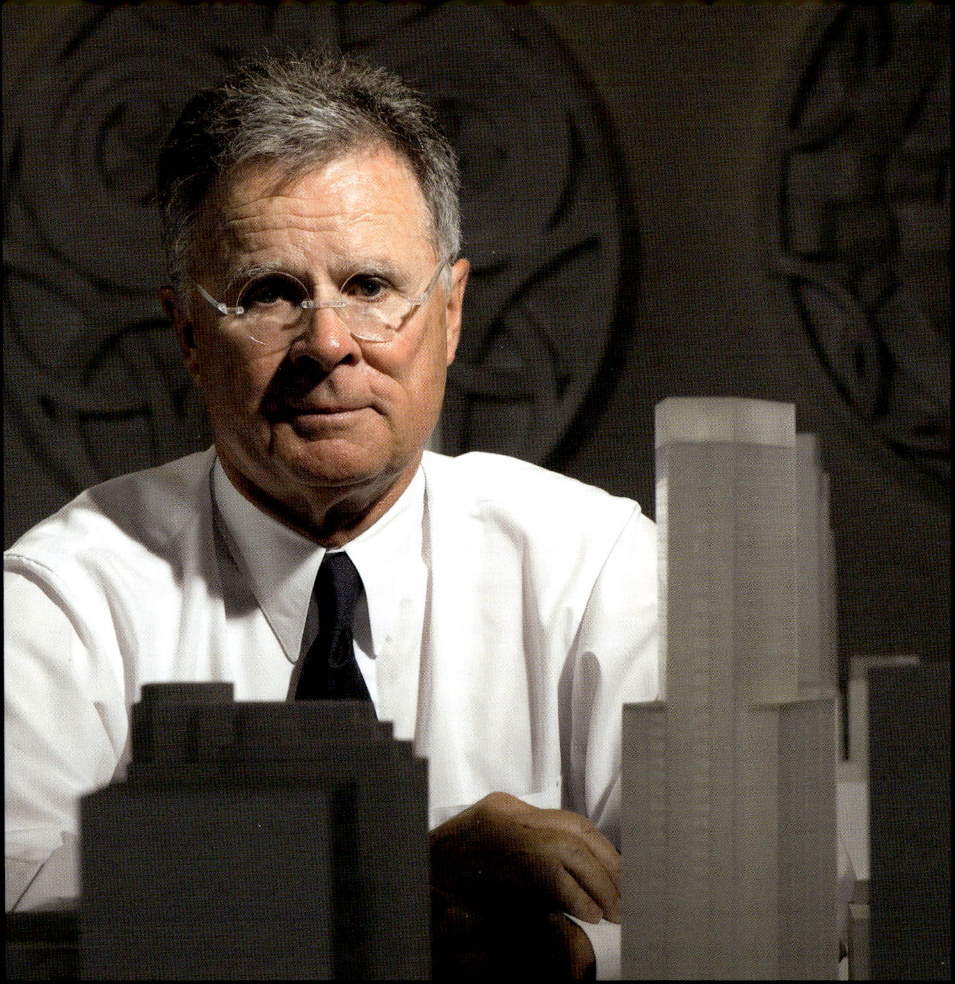

Foreword

Beauty Is a Noun: Thoughts on Modern Architecture

By Laurence Booth

Modernism has been the dominant architectural style for my entire professional life. Stripped of ornament, its bare bones exposed, the modernist approach claimed the cultural high ground for most of the 20th century.

Modernism was thought to represent technological and industrial progress. Flush surfaces eliminated ornamental detail. Proportion was replaced by function. Harmony and balance were overshadowed by idiosyncratic form. Most modernists, meanwhile, thought little of culture and almost nothing of the broad spirit of architecture. Beauty for its own sake was for sissies.

My career in architecture has been spent challenging the status quo. I can trace this back to my father's practice as a patent attorney, a profession in which innovation is the norm. In school, as minimalism was typically pushed as doctrine, I was drawn instead to the work of Brunelleschi, Palladio and others identified with the Italian Renaissance. For me, architecture was more than matching technology to function. It was also about creating form as an expression of humanism.

After graduating from MIT, I spent two years in the U.S. Army stationed in Munich, West Germany with the 24th Infantry Division. My discharge in Europe allowed me to take several months traveling the Continent in a VW minibus with my wife Pat and young son Fenton. Our Grand Tour provided a capstone to my education. And it revealed to me that modernism alone was inadequate to the architectural task ahead.

Starting my own practice in Chicago in 1966 brought me in close touch with Sullivan, Root, Burnham, Wright and Mies. Their buildings are classics in many ways, and their beauty has stood the test of time. Carson Pirie Scott, The Rookery, the Reliance Building, Robie House and even the modernist Crown Hall—they are all so different from one another, and each unique, beautiful and poetic.

Architecture has always been collaborative, and appropriately, many people are behind the work that is profiled in this book. Thanks go to clients who are key team members in any project, also to my dedicated architectural colleagues, brilliant contractors, consultants and craftspeople. To communicate these lessons I collaborated closely with writer Jay Pridmore and graphic designer Sandro Franchini. Heartfelt thanks also to my family, Pat, Fenton, Victoria, Adriene and Ted. They have been supportive and patient over all these years of searching for the next beautiful building.

Architecture often blends familiarity and surprise, utility and emotion.

Introduction
Modern Beyond Style

Life stories often involve paradox if not contradiction, and two valid observations about the career of architect Larry Booth appear at odds with one another. The first and most apparent is that Larry is a designer of remarkable creativity. For fifty years he and his firm have created innovative buildings in multiple typologies with striking and surprising results. Another clear attribute of Larry's architecture, and that of his firm Booth Hansen, is a strongly systematic process as the elements of design are assembled to create functional buildings.

Creativity and process are not contradictory, but nor do they always go together. The success of Larry Booth as an architect and founder of a leading Chicago firm demonstrates that the two can, and often should, be wedded in an architecture that strives for both efficiency and beauty.

One can readily witness both sides in Larry's work. It was true early in his career when he was largely a modernist who created well-ordered buildings, while also exhibiting originality. As he reached mid-career, his search for something new led him to experiment with historical forms, touching on post-modernism while never abandoning the rational predisposition of the modern.

As Larry and his firm matured, he used his ability to blend functional and artistic ideas on the larger canvas of institutional buildings and tall urban structures. Working at this scale, economics and construction technology increased the complexity of his architecture. But the approach, as seen in the sculptural School of the Art Institute dormitory in the Loop, and directly across State Street in the rationalist Joffrey Tower, is always to assemble diverse ideas in fresh, inventive ways unmarked by any predefined style.

In a 2005 article on Larry's career, a client was quoted that it is hard to put your finger on what marks a Larry Booth building. "But you just know it." In fact, the difficulty in defining Booth Hansen work is ultimately its greatest asset. One concludes that he and his office are free of superficial expectations of style, and have remarkable freedom in discovering a new and optimal design for any project.

Booth buildings are typically a mix of familiarity and innovation. They rarely challenge the senses. A house looks like a home. A skyscraper looks like it belongs where it is. But they always have touches, sometimes subtle, that call attention that this design is different from what's been done before. It's often a feature that addresses a unique need—to preserve the environment in a special way, or employ an economic new technology.

One could say that Larry has been a precursor, as his longtime approach to architecture has become well accepted in the 21st century. The best architecture of our current time blends the imagery of art and technology, for example, or the past with the present. It typically creates modern flowing space fused with touches of tradition.

Larry's work and that of Booth Hansen follow no doctrine. Rather it is inspired by the phrase that Larry often uses to describe his work: "modern beyond style."

The Ann Halsted Rowhouses in Lincoln Park, designed by Louis Sullivan, represented an early project for arry in which he updated living space inside an iconic work of 19th century architecture.

Beginnings
The Arc of History

The Rookery, Burnham & Root Architects, Chicago, Illinois, 1888 (with a 1905 remodeling by Frank Lloyd Wright).

Laurence O. Booth was born in 1936 and raised in LaGrange, Illinois, a suburb of Chicago. He became familiar with Chicago's architectural riches early in his life, as he occasionally accompanied his father, a patent attorney, to his office which was in The Rookery, one of the great buildings of the old Chicago School with its airy atrium and dramatic spiral staircase.

Design came naturally to the young man, perhaps influenced by the drawings attached to the patents that his father brought into the world. Larry also had a proclivity for building things, mostly from wood, often pieces of furniture, and sometimes as he got older he created objects that were purely sculptural. As for his future, he was hardly sure what he wanted. But by the time he chose a college, Stanford University looked like the best fit. Architecture students were in the College of Arts and Sciences where Larry got a liberal education while he also learned about practical design.

Stanford was a good choice. His aesthetic sense was sharpened in studio classes where he drew imagined buildings and could also experiment with sculpture. In both architecture and art he developed an interest in relationships of geometric form.

There was something else at Stanford that was key, and that was engineering courses which Larry took, somewhat to satisfy his father who was sure that technical skills would pay off in the long run. In those classes, an important influence was professor John E. Arnold, a pioneer in what was called "creative engineering." Arnold believed that technical people could benefit from inventive thinking, that when faced with a problem, the successful solution might be something never done before. Arnold thought in terms of process and encouraged students—also advised companies for whom the professor consulted—to organize their thinking in a way to enhance creativity. He identified phases of the creative process which, broadly speaking, included analysis, synthesis and evaluation.

Arnold's ideas were well received among some architects, especially in the Bay Area where William Wurster and Theodore Bernardi had developed a regional modernism with indigenous materials and an Arts and Crafts approach. Arnold's influence included his conviction that design, architectural or otherwise, should address "human values and the needs of society." More modestly, architects should consider the preferences of the client in any project, which, bluntly speaking, were not high on the list of European-inspired modernists. But thinking of how people used buildings and how they would feel inside—this struck some California architects as a natural link between form and function.

After graduation, Larry started graduate school in architecture at Harvard where modernism was pervasive. Function was industrial.

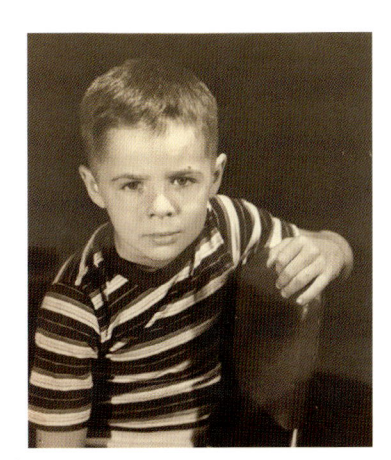

The architect as a kid.

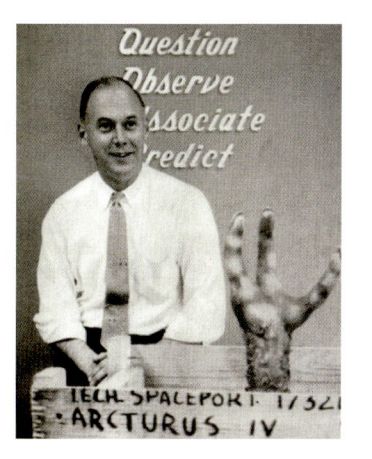

John Arnold, the creativity theorist who influenced Larry at Stanford.

13

The entry to the MIT campus reflects a noble past. The school's architecture program embraced Larry's belief that buildings can elicit emotion drawn from history, a possibility that he found lacking in Harvard's strictly modernist approach.

Beauty was perceived as the harmonious pairing of rational construction for a specific purpose. Ornamentation had been squeezed out.

What he quickly perceived as missing was the idea that the California group never forgot: humanism. That meant emotional comfort as a valid function, and that a measure of ornament enhanced good design. Larry's first studio class at Harvard made it clear, unfortunately, that these things were unwelcome. Shingles, a traditional material, were out. Colorful treatments were anathema. And then there was the option of a pitched roof which seemed entirely practical to shed rain or snow. Pitched roofs were verboten at Harvard, and it did not take long for the professors who passed by Larry's drawing board to criticize any roof he drew with even a shallow slope.

The last straw came late in the first semester when a professor called Larry in to ask why he had not "joined the program." The professor's belief, and Harvard's, was that the Bauhaus style could solve every architectural problem. Larry replied that traditional architecture had already solved many problems, and to neglect it seemed… well… The meeting ended with no common ground. Larry was unsure what to do.

Larry returned to his dorm. Distraught, he thought of a book that he enjoyed, *The Architecture of America: A Social and Cultural History*. It analyzed the nation's architectural history as a reflection of changing cultural forces. Seen in this way, any one building was an interpreter of many influences. This made sense to Larry, who noticed that one of the book's authors, Albert Bush-Brown, taught in the architecture school at MIT. Larry called him. He got an invitation to come over to that campus, a mile or so from Harvard, for a visit.

Bush-Brown was friendly, and as open to Larry in this visit as he was to different kinds of architecture in his book. They talked about California and the regional architecture that evolved there. One architect that interested both of them was Bernard Maybeck, the early modernist from California who believed that the natural world could be enhanced by architecture, and who had no problem with ornamental touches. Bush-Brown said that perhaps Larry should consider transferring to MIT. Larry decided to do so, and in the second semester (while staying in his Harvard dorm) he found a more amenable program on the other side of Cambridge.

MIT was one of the oldest architecture schools in the country. It was initially modeled after the École des Beaux-Arts, and while its teaching had moved toward the modern, as all schools did in this period, it retained elements of the old. What turned out to be an eclectic approach was fine with Larry. In fact, William Wurster himself had been dean at MIT in the 1940s. The current dean, Pietro Belluschi, was a modernist who would go on to work on the Pan Am Building and Lincoln Center in New York. But there was a certain freedom in the studio courses. Among Larry's teachers was Kenzo Tange, a modernist as well, but one with an expressive streak (later seen in his gymnasium for the 1964 Tokyo Olympics).

Tange taught not with dogma but with questions. "What are you trying to do here?" he'd ask when critiquing a design. The professor judged student projects based on how well various elements seemed to work, and he would propose alternatives that might be incorporated. Tange's mentorship taught what Larry soon regarded as the first rule of architecture: that there are many possible approaches to any design. Another Tange lesson was implied by what the professor did not say. He never promoted a specific style, style being the fraught concept which Larry came to regard as a limitation.

After a year and a half at MIT, Larry had a professional degree and well-rounded perspective on what was possible in architecture. He embraced some lessons in modernism including the precise rationalism of Mies van der Rohe. He was interested in Pierluigi Nervi of Rome, a master of reinforced concrete. On the MIT campus, another towering modernist, Eero Saarinen, had recently designed two major structures, totally different from one another, Kresge Auditorium and MIT Chapel. And then there was Leonardo Ricci, a professor in the program, whose designs ranged from limestone houses that appeared tied to the earth, to futuristic designs that seemed born of Fritz Lang's film *Metropolis*.

After MIT, Larry had an obligation to the U.S. Army, as a portion of his education was financed by ROTC. His job in the service while

Larry with Kenzo Tange at MIT.

Walter Netsch of SOM who invented the system which he called "field theory."

stationed in West Germany had very little to do with architecture or design. But it did give him free time to travel around Central Europe, which was filled with the kind of architectural landmarks that many modernists had made a point of rejecting. He toured baroque palaces like the Würzburg Residenz and wondered why modernists would term their theatricality "dishonest."

Europe was a continuous discovery for the architect-to-be, and when he was discharged, he embarked with his wife Pat and toddler son on a Grand Tour, post-war style. They did not neglect the modern, as they saw the landmarks of Le Corbusier and Mies's early brick houses in Germany. They went to Italy and saw the amazing range of architecture in that country, including the villas of Palladio in the provinces outside Venice. As Larry took them in, he thought of the harmonic ratios—the Golden Section—that they supposedly reflected. And inside, he could not help but notice the light that filtered through successions of space, not too different from some of the best modern architecture that he'd seen.

Toward the end of their tour, they arrived in Athens to experience the Acropolis. Nearby they also looked at modern works in the ancient capital such as the American Embassy, designed by Walter Gropius. The Gropius design impressed him for the repose that modernism could render, also for its proportions which appeared to be inspired by the classical.

While touring around the steps of the Athens embassy, Larry and his wife noticed another American couple doing the same thing. They were Walter and Dawn Clark Netsch, also of Chicago. Walter was already well-known as a partner at Skidmore Owings and Merrill, having recently designed one of his signature works, the Air Force Academy in Colorado Springs. Larry introduced himself. Walter told him that he should come for a visit and maybe a job at SOM when they were home. The chance encounter motivated Larry to learn something of Netsch's approach to architecture, called "field theory," a system to create architectural form through the repetitive rotation of simple geometric shapes. It was an interesting idea, Larry discerned, for its ability to achieve an important goal of all architecture. That was to create order in complexity.

Europe was a discovery for Larry, also an affirmation that architecture had taken many varied forms over the course of history. He saw the need for originality, but he also saw that the modern could be inspired by the traditional. As Larry headed home to begin his career, he was eager to put into practice the ideas collected in the classroom and in his travels. He knew it would take time to formulate a vision, but he was ready to start.

Larry's interest in Palladio was rare in modernist-trained architects in 1973 when he gave this lecture at the Miesian sanctuary, Illinois Institute of Technology.

REGINA VIRTUS

PALLADIAN VILLAS
FOUR HUNDRED YEARS OF
EXCELLENCE & INFLUENCE

An Illustrated Lecture By
LAURENCE BOOTH, AIA

Thursday, Nov. 1, 12:30 p.m.
CRAWFORD AUDITORIUM
10 West 32nd Street, Chicago

SCHOOL OF ARCHITECTURE & PLANNING
ILLINOIS INSTITUTE OF TECHNOLOGY

Larry's untitled plexiglass sculpture, c. 1962, was an experiment in the relationship between the simple and the complex.

System
Ordering the Real World

The Five, with Larry at left, who were artists who sought order in abstraction.

When he returned to Chicago from Europe, Larry visited his acquaintance Walter Netsch and found that Netsch's firm, SOM, was not hiring at that moment. Instead, Netsch suggested that Larry go see an architect who had recently left SOM and was now on his own. Stanley Tigerman was young and serious, and was seeking help. Tigerman hired Larry as his first employee, and Larry's few years with Tigerman, who later became a leading Chicago architect, were notable for at least two reasons. One was that Tigerman was a severe taskmaster, related less to long hours and more to the design rigor of work that came out of his office.

Tigerman's commissions were mostly rehabs and townhouses, most not too large. Yet no detail was too small for the closest attention. Proportions should be classically perfect, and materials appropriate. If some of Tigerman's values were subjective (he became a notorious architectural scold) others were objective and highly disciplined. If a bead in the millwork or the placement of an electric outlet was wrong, all hell broke loose. Precision, Tigerman insisted, is what separates design excellence from the commonplace.

Another benefit in working for Tigerman was that his practice was active in Chicago's Lincoln Park community, North Side neighborhoods that had seen better days but were on the cusp of a renaissance. That meant plenty of work for architects, and especially those able to harmonize with the traditional lines of existing buildings. Tigerman (a Yale graduate) and Larry, along with another Tigerman employee, Jim Nagle (like Larry from Stanford and MIT), had been trained that modernism was up-to-date and fashionable. The challenge in Lincoln Park was to blend modern design in the historical context.

A Tigerman project, a townhouse complex called Pickwick Village, was an example. Pickwick's modernity was designed to cohere with older buildings in the immediate area in terms of material (mostly brick) and proportion (including uniform rooflines). Other Tigerman projects in that period included renovations in which Larry spent considerable time measuring existing structures. Measuring each and every dimension "was a brilliant teaching tool" whether Tigerman intended it to be or not, Larry said in an oral history interview in 2000. "It makes you look at details... a very intense way to look at buildings."

Young architects normally enter the profession with more energy than can be expended on entry-level jobs. So Larry satisfied his creativity beyond the Tigerman studio with a serious interest in art. As a sculptor he became identified with a group of young abstract artists called The Five. Larry's work, mostly reliefs in plexiglass, used simple forms like squares and triangles to compose complex

Larry was second from left at a panel discussion with Tom Beeby speaking and Stanley Tigerman seated beside the podium.

In the Chicago Architects *exhibit catalogue, Larry Booth was included among several generations of architects, pictured on the cover, top row, sixth from left.*

objects... or alternatively he reduced complex objects to simple form. Abstract art, he said in a statement for an exhibition in 1968, was "a search for the synthesis of the universal/eternal... with the individual/personal."

In 1966, Larry left Tigerman's office and went off to start his own firm with Jim Nagle. They stayed busy with rehab projects, largely in Lincoln Park where one of the more interesting ones was the renovation of a kitchen in a house originally designed by Louis Sullivan. Renovation meant mixing modern elements with old ones, a process which revealed to Larry that design need not be static, rather, like nature, it could grow over time.

As Booth & Nagle located themselves in an office in the Fine Arts Building on South Michigan Avenue, each worked largely on his own projects and in his own way. Nagle tended to work silently, and once his idea was established, sought to complete it single-mindedly. Larry on the other hand was talkative with clients, colleagues and others, and he customarily approached design by proposing multiple alternatives to present to clients, to discuss and modify.

Around 1970, Larry met industrial designer John Massey, head of the Center for Advanced Research in Design. Massey told him of a project that he might want to join, a commission for Atlantic Richfield Company (ARCO) to create a modern filling station. The Center, a creation of Container Corporation, was dedicated to the study and realization of all types of corporate design projects. For the ARCO commission, Massey assembled a team with engineers, marketing people, graphic designers, and others in addition to the architect.

The project began with the team making a long list of what the design should achieve, then systematically proposing forms that achieved multiple objectives. For Larry it was an example of how architecture could use basic geometry, in this case the triangle, manipulated to satisfy an array of needs. Its success suggested to him that a systematic approach was appropriate to architecture of many kinds.

In 1976 came another milestone in Larry's career prompted by an exhibit entitled *100 Years of Architecture in Chicago*. Curated in Germany, it had opened in Europe. It was based on the idea that Chicago became modernism's epicenter primarily, if not exclusively, because the Chicago School of the 19th century had evolved into the Miesian "less is more" of the 20th.

Some architects found this interpretation limited if not outrageous as it neglected many other giants of architecture. "What are we going to do about this?" Tigerman barked to Larry and other young architects when they met, as they often did. Ironically,

Stanley Tigerman.

Larry's ARCO station was included in the German show, but he also believed, like Tigerman, that many other Chicago buildings deserved attention. They conceived a counter-exhibition entitled *Chicago Architects*, with more than 100 excellent works in diverse styles, from the classical Museum of Science and Industry to the proto-solar designs of Keck and Keck built at the 1933 World's Fair.

Chicago Architects and *100 Years of Architecture in Chicago* opened simultaneously, the latter in the Museum of Contemporary Art, the former in the lobby of Harry Weese's Time-Life Building nearby. The result of the "collision of architectural ideas," as *Tribune* critic Paul Gapp called it, was a demonstration that serious architecture in Chicago followed many paths. *The New York Times* celebrated its "qualities of pluralism."

The *Chicago Architects* organizers were pleased by the shake-up, and it inspired them to plan more exhibits. They christened their group the "Chicago Seven," a take-off on the conspiracy trial after the 1968 Democratic Convention. Besides Tigerman and Booth, it included Stuart Cohen, Jim Nagle, Ben Weese, Tom Beeby and James Ingo Freed. (The addition of others, including Helmut Jahn, Jerry Horn and Ken Schroeder, did not move them to change the name.) Their message was that Miesian architecture had developed an authoritarian streak to be resisted.

In 1977, the Seven staged another exhibit, this one with new designs of Chicago townhouses. Called *The Exquisite Corpse*, it was named after the Surrealist parlor game in which artists composed a human figure, each by adding an arm, a torso or leg without knowing what others had done. The exhibit had each member of the group design a townhouse for a typical Chicago city lot, to show how different seven independent designs could be.

A *Tribune* article about the show was headlined, "Whimsy Rules Design Show." To Larry, that missed the point. His townhouse, which he said was inspired by the theologian Teilhard de Chardin who believed in the inherent harmonies of the universe, had an interior which flowed with modernist ease through four stories and ended with a chapel at the top. Larry explained his design by writing that "architecture could be connected to these important ideas that we deal with in terms of understanding our surroundings and our experiences in the late twentieth century." At this point in his career, Larry was learning to capture harmonious form. His search for ideas was beginning.

The Exquisite Corpse was an exhibit of imagined Chicago townhouses both innovative and harmonious with older neighbors. Larry's contribution has frosted glass, second from left.

Kemper Hall

Unbuilt Project, Kenosha, Wisconsin, 1968

For an Episcopal girls' preparatory school, Booth & Nagle designed what was essentially an experimental design which would enable the campus to grow and change with maximum ease as time passed and needs shifted. Using a plan of squares and isosceles triangles, the design fits into a series of 22 ft. x 22 ft. bays. The configuration of the elements only seems random. Their placement is "related to recent developments in bio-molecular research," Larry told *Architectural Forum*, which covered the unbuilt project. His implication was that the project was designed with a view to organic growth over time. The size of the bays, to be executed in reinforced concrete, was selected with an eye to the different functions which might be served by dividing some spaces for specific functions and combining others.

The idea for the Kemper Hall project appeared similar to the "field theory" of SOM's Walter Netsch, which fundamentally assembled rotating squares and cubes to create structures of individuality and inherent unity. As for Kemper Hall, Larry was aware that its 19th century main school building possessed its own manipulation of basic geometric units, as Gothic and Gothic Revival buildings do. Thus, the seeming clash of the old and the new would be softened by time, and by the beholder's eye which would gradually absorb the underlying principle shared by traditional and modern architecture.

Repetitious geometry is made to conform to the unique lakefront site.

The building was designed so that it could be enlarged in any direction without disturbing the architecture. Interiors can be opened and closed easily as needs change.

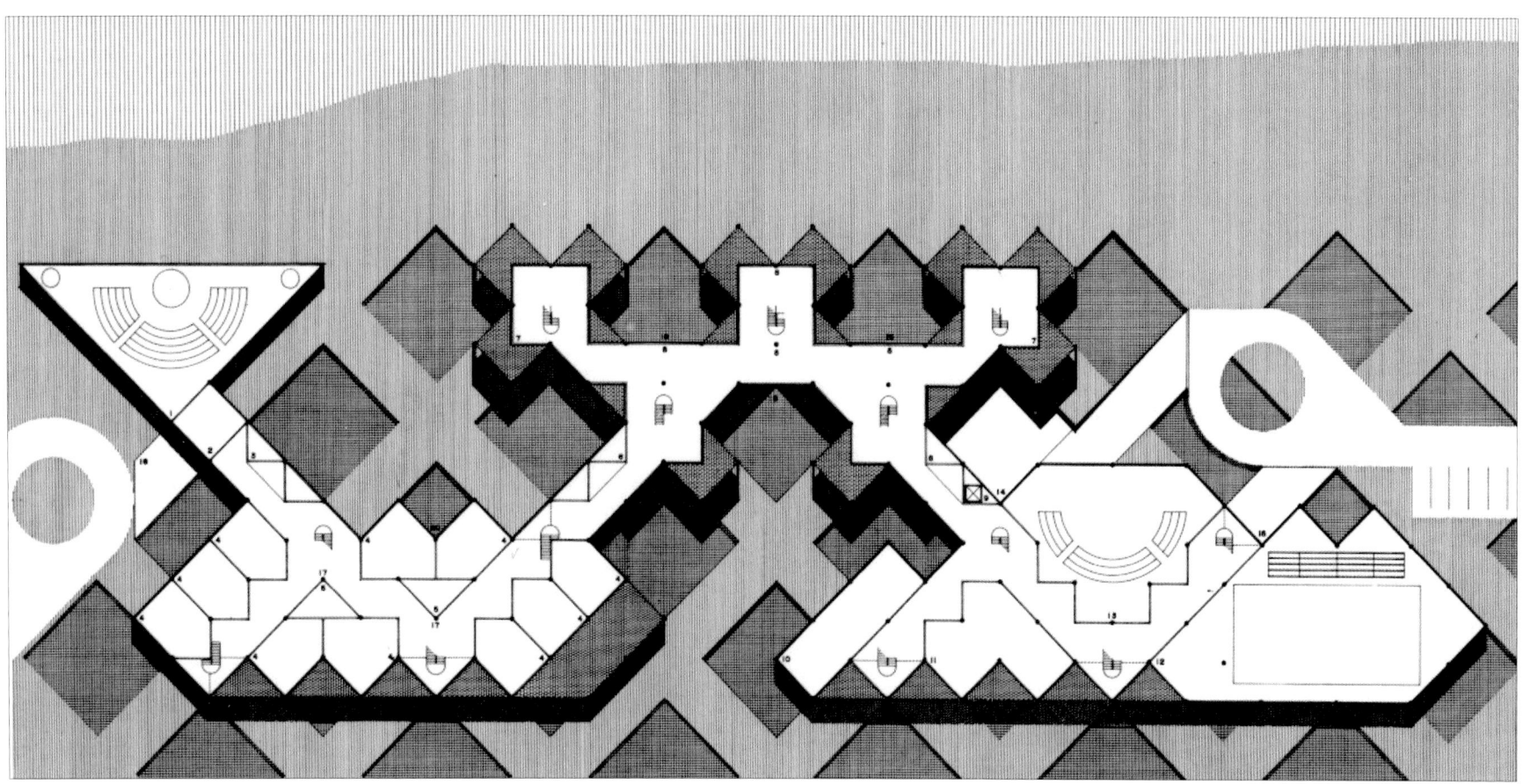

ARCO Service Station

Illinois (various locations), 1969

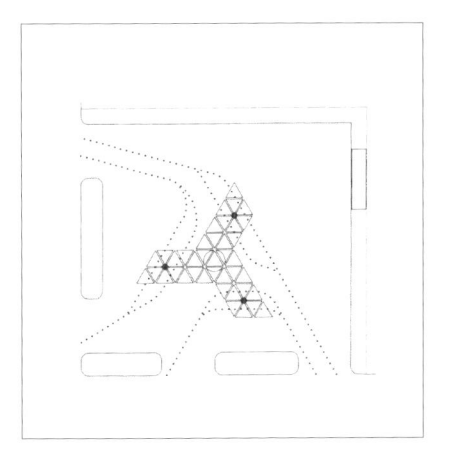

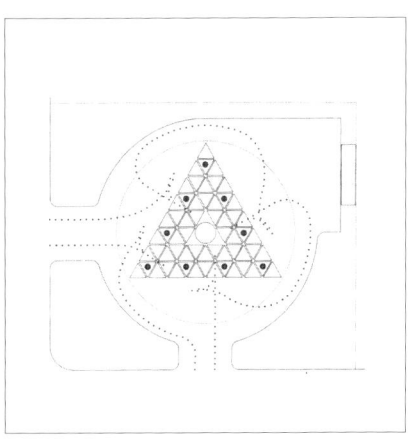

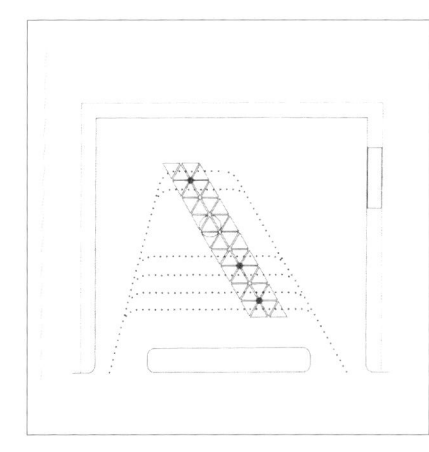

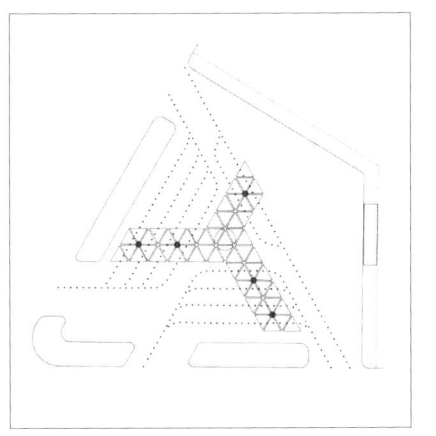

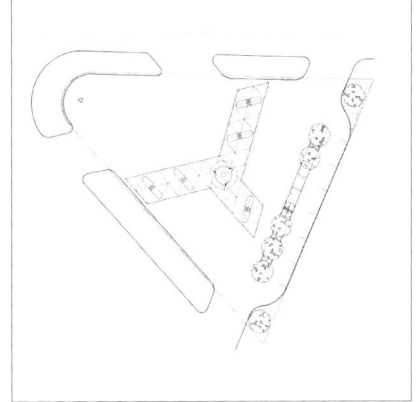

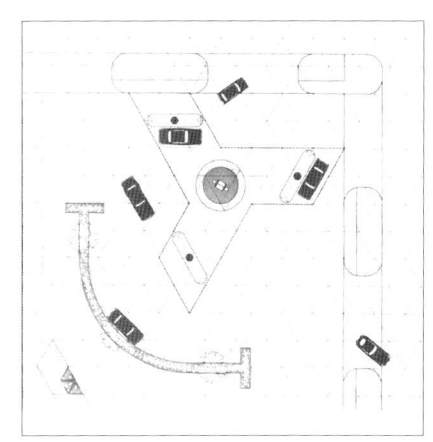

Varied configurations show that the system accommodates many sites.

Modernist architecture placed the highest value on rational design in the 1960s when the Center for Advanced Research and Design, created by the Chicago-based Container Corporation, assembled an interdisciplinary team to design the most modern and efficient service station possible. Larry was the architect of the group that also included graphic designers, product designers and marketing specialists. The approach sought to create form to meet an array of requirements for the client, Atlantic Richfield Corporation.

As attributes of construction, circulation, branding, sales and other conditions were listed, data was fed into a mainframe computer. The output suggested which design elements could meet multiple needs, and it guided design decisions related to siting, materials and even details such as the number of pumps at the station and their spacing. The geometric profile of the ARCO station, characterized by equilateral triangles, was neither arbitrary nor accidental. It suited the siting of the facility on a corner. It used common steel materials for economy and a basic construction system for efficiency.

A modular system creates interesting profiles with an exceedingly simple construction.

Barglow House
Chicago, 1969

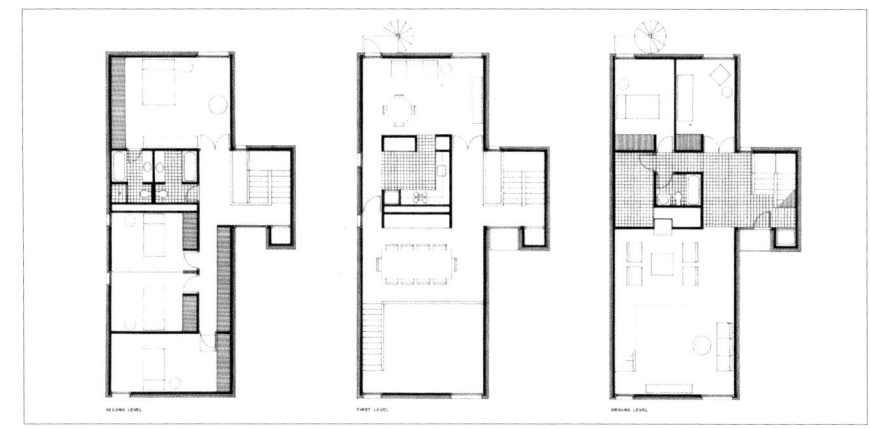

The Barglow House on the South Side of Chicago was designed for a neighborhood that was once splendid, had fallen on hard times, and was being revitalized, a process that has since been completed. In this case, Larry used tenets of modernism in judicious ways in a house that received an honor award by *Architectural Record*, which was the bible of the modernist movement.

The house uses a limited material palette, largely of brick piers and plate glass, in creating a form that was geometrically unique, also meeting the needs for protection with solid walls and recessed windows. Inside, it is underdetailed and provides large interior space and walls for large works of modern art. The main ornament of the interior lies in the beauty of simple materials and craftsmanship, as in the parquet floor and open staircase.

A key aspect of the success of the Barglow House was something that was not evident in the photos that were submitted for the *AR* award, and that is its compatibility with the older and traditional homes of the neighborhood. By cleaving to the proportions and materiality of the Georgian and Victorian structures of the neighborhood, the Barglow House demonstrates that modern architecture, carefully wrought, can be harmonious with most other styles of architecture, equally well designed.

Brick piers suggest strength. Plate glass provides openness.

Simple materials and plain surfaces render a luxurious feel.

The Atrium

Elmhurst, Illinois, 1971

By 1971, architects who found rectilinear modernism monotonous found developers who agreed. That was the impulse was behind The Atrium townhouse and condominium project in Elmhurst. It was the first planned unit development in Elmhurst, and an effort to modify the typical rank and file of suburban houses.

Orientations and floor plans are organized so that houses benefit as much as possible from natural sunlight and long views from the houses to exterior space and common landscape elements. The architecture features oblique angles in floor plans and elevations. The modernity of the development at large is highlighted in the design of the central clubhouse, a focal point both visually and socially for The Atrium. It features dynamic geometry with abundant natural light and interlocking spaces within.

The Atrium clubhouse uses geometry to signal a variety of uses inside.

Modern window walls and solar orientation are among modern elements.

Barr House

Hinsdale, Illinois, 1974

The Barr House won significant praise when built because of its sharp exterior surfaces and the elegance of the interior. These were achieved through the architect's command of geometry which is taken nearly to an experimental limit. While Larry claimed in several articles on the house that it was a traditional American design, transformed, it incorporates at least two overlapping floor plans, one superimposed at a 45-degree angle over another. The result is an array of overlapping, interlocking spaces.

As if to highlight the geometry, the color and texture palette is limited. Along with the design's horizontal movement, double-high volumes create vertical views which extend through skylights. Living spaces in the Barr House involve a "complex experience of space and light," as Larry put it, adding that the house requires little in the way of wall decoration, as the light and shadow are constantly shifting.

The placement of the Barr House provides sight lights in many directions.

Opposite page: The design interprets the modernist concept of universal space.

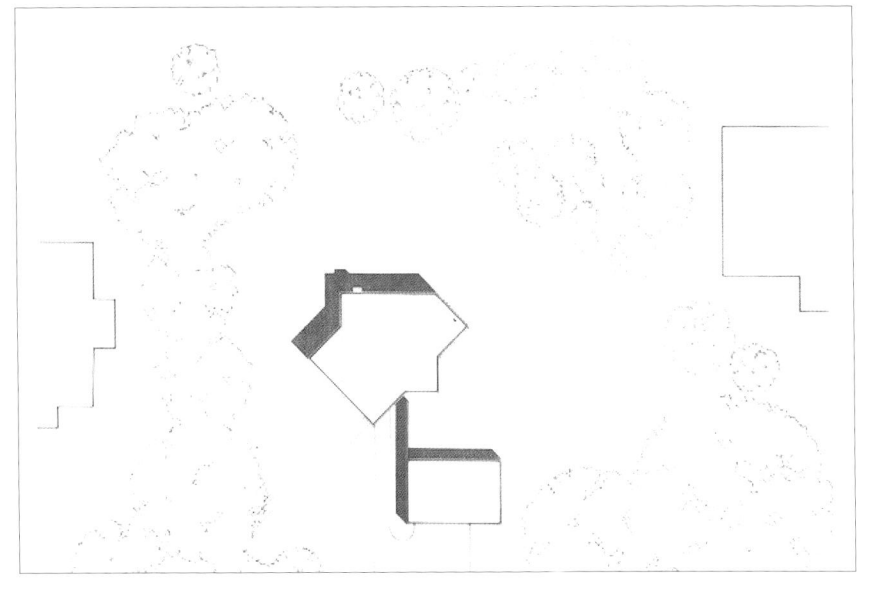

31

Magnuson House
Vashon Island, Washington, 1974

Bridge provides access over the slope and through the woods.

Magnuson House features deceptively complex geometry.

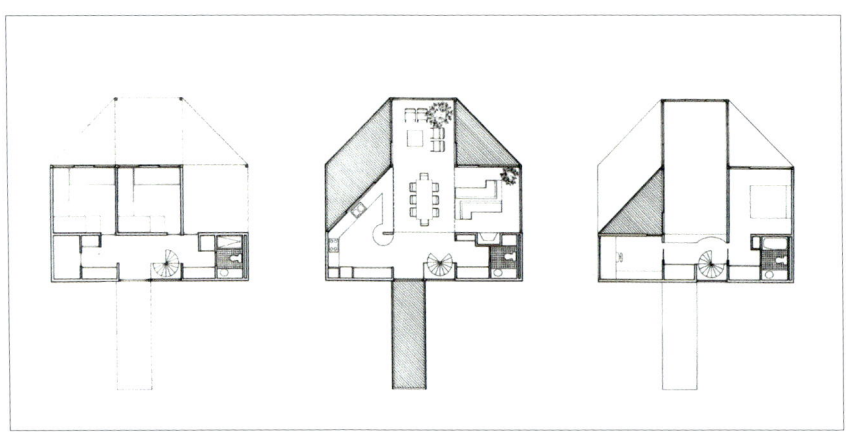

What is clear of the De Stijl movement, which influenced European and American art starting in the early 20th century, is that any single work represents but a portion of the universal whole. When Larry was presented with the wooded site on an island in Puget Sound, his objective was to create a structure to become a harmonious portion of the larger environment. The primary colors and simple geometry of De Stijl provided a system to accomplish that.

The gentle asymmetry of the Magnuson design harmonizes with the terrain and the forest, as does the use of a timber frame and wood cladding inside and out. The vertical feel of the exterior is amplified inside with double-high spaces, a balconied upper floor, and large glass walls and clerestories that provide sightlines to the treetops.

This was a rare foray for Booth & Nagle into the Pacific Northwest. It was also rare for Larry to adopt what would be viewed as a so-called style, though De Stijl was a loose template. But Larry discerned patterns, albeit complex ones, in the terrain, and he simplified them with a system that featured both clear simplicity and wide-ranging flexibility in the result.

Interior reveals Mondrianesque order, which is also suggested by the irregular grid of the elevation.

Fox House
Glencoe, Illinois, 1977

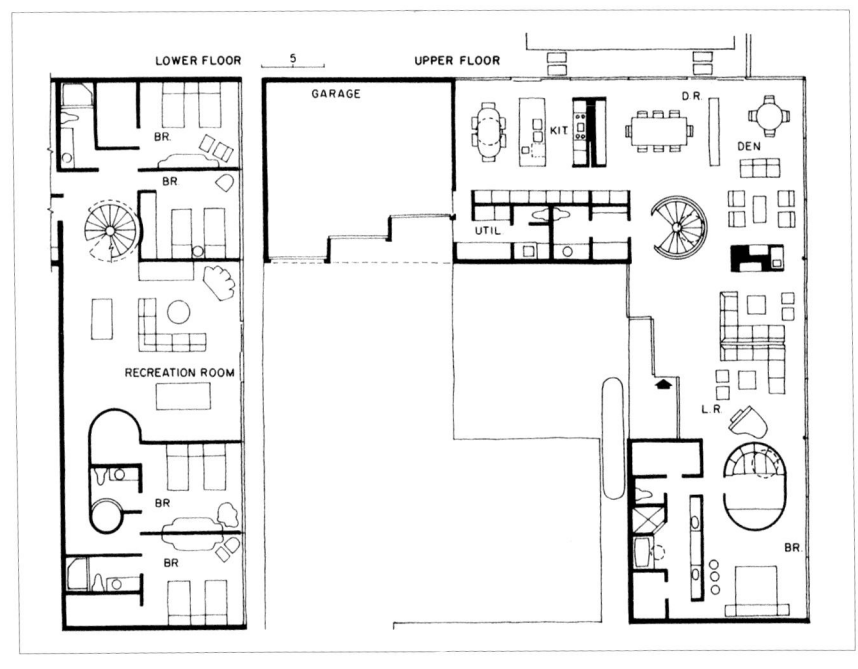

The Foxes did not look at first like clients who would inhabit a stripped down modernist house. They were moving from a traditional home filled with antiques. But they were downsizing and determined to simplify their lives, as they told Larry in early interviews. But as Larry understood the Foxes, and as the Foxes understood how an ideal home might be designed, they concluded that the result might be minimal and even Miesian.

The site was an exceptional perch between a Lake Michigan bluff and a ravine. Clearly, the setting was the "big idea" of the design—with views, the changing light as it filtered through trees, and the relatively steep pitch down to the beach. Designing the house was primarily an exercise to create interior spaces with visual access to nature. These could be on two levels, the main floor with living and dining space plus a master bedroom, and a lower story with bedrooms that open fully to the bluff. From the front door, the house looks like "a modern ranch house, one story, nothing more," Mrs. Fox said with satisfaction.

Opening the house as much as possible to the outdoors did not exclude an architectural sense of place. The grid of the house is clear if not emphatic, and one senses this order especially in the entry and before the views open up through the glass back wall. There is also a certain richness of material, and not least the travertine floors, paved diagonally. Mrs. Fox was pleased to have found the travertine herself, and that stone affirmed Larry's notion, shared by Miesians, that richness resides in undisguised materials.

Fox House is sited between Lake Michigan and a steep ravine.

Benefits of the site include abundant natural light and panoramic views.

Museum of Contemporary Art

Chicago, 1978

The commission to create an enlarged Museum of Contemporary Art on Chicago's Near North Side was an exercise in knitting together two older buildings and creating a modern structure worthy of the city's architectural tradition. Exterior form-making began by comprehending the respective scales of the two, a former bakery and a townhouse. The massing of each is broken down into the square aluminum panels that uniformly clad the entire museum. Connecting the two sides is a "bridge" of a triangular truss and glass. This became the outermost gallery among several layered in the interior.

The glassy facade and a ramp to the front door provide an inviting entry to the museum, replacing the private and unapproachable feel of both buildings before the renovation. An early design for this project appeared inspired by the Pompidou Center in Paris; a high-tech appearance plus bright colors were toned down in deference to a conservative impulse on the part of the trustees, who were nonetheless devotees of modern art. "It is less Beaubourg, more [Chicago-style] structural expression," said architect Stuart Cohen in a review of the building in 1979.

The opening exhibit in the new MCA was titled *The Reborn Building: New Uses, Old Places*, which highlighted the federal General Service Administration's acknowledgement and participation in the then-fledgling historic preservation movement.

Left: Openness of both the street outside and galleries within marked the city's then-new museum.

Below: Sketches for the MCA design.

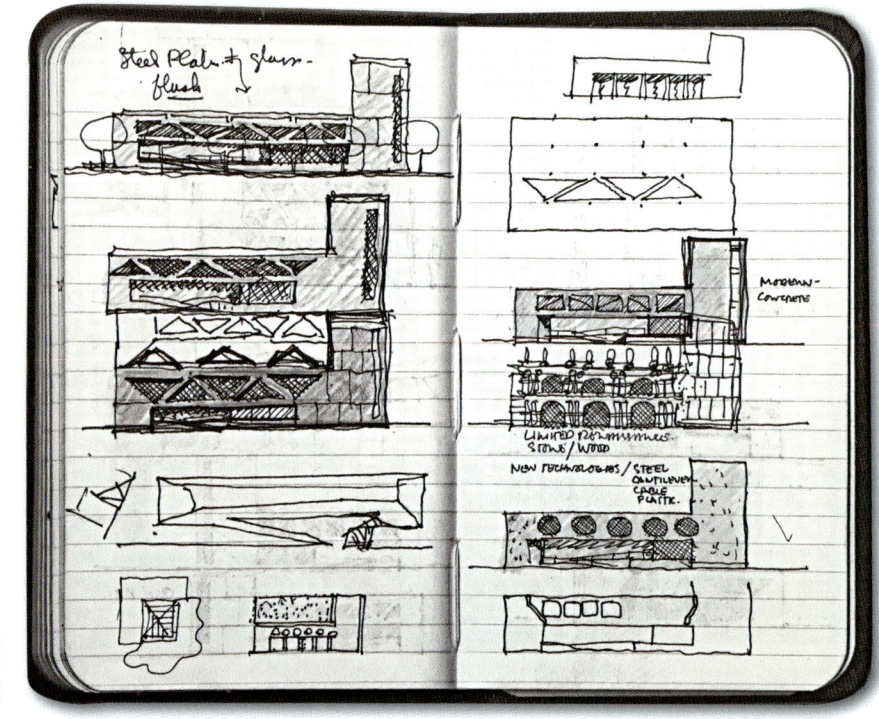

The Museum of Contemporary Art was essentially a bridge between two older buildings.

The Booth Hansen studio on Hubbard Street, 1980's

Process
Setting Goals and Building a Team

After *The Exquisite Corpse* exhibit, Larry became increasingly skilled at blending modern forms with traditional ones. His practice expanded at this time as well, and it was not by mere coincidence that he became determined to develop a more organized and predictable methodology. He sought an ingrained process that could apply to a greater volume of work, also to an expanded design repertoire.

Many modern architects, Larry believed, dismissed the notion of process. He had seen other studios that seemed intentionally chaotic as they cast around for a brilliant idea. Larry rejected that approach, and as he matured as an architect, he found himself doing more of what John Arnold and his Stanford professors taught. That was to clarify the requirements of a project, then distill elements, assemble and refine. As Larry had long done, moreover, he made it a practice to present three alternative approaches, a step which challenged his creativity and also enriched interaction with the client.

As the Booth Hansen process evolved, it took a significant step forward during a small commission in 1984 for the Indian Hill Country Club in Winnetka. The assignment was to add a library to the rambling Federal-style clubhouse which had been originally built in 1914. As Larry met with members of the committee responsible for the project, they talked about the many things they wanted, including a desire to retain the farmhouse feel of the building and its unpretentious charm.

Larry took all this in, then talked with the committee chairman. Larry reviewed what he had heard, and the chairman, who was in the advertising business, replied with a suggestion that stuck. "Why don't you make a list," he said. "In advertising we call it the 'goals board.'" That made it clear which objectives were harmonious with one another, and which were conflictual. Writing down objectives was hardly a stunning discovery, but getting them on a display board for everyone on the design team to see was a step that many architects were too impatient to take.

For some time, Larry had been convinced that the ideal design process could be used for all commissions regardless of size or typology. What came shortly thereafter was a project that was sprawling in scale and for which an organized process was critical. That was the rehabilitation of Printer's Row, a stretch of Dearborn Street on Chicago's Near South Side.

The Printer's Row idea, which triggered a renaissance in a neglected section on the edge of downtown, was conceived when Larry was on a flight with Harry Weese, and he told the older Weese that he was interested in reviving old buildings on the several decrepit blocks just south of the Loop. Weese, a leading modernist at the time, and who was also drawn to historic preservation, was interested. Over the next year or so, Larry and Weese put together a group.

Harry Weese, the modernist who championed the restoration of Printer's Row.

A sketch by Harry Weese of the reimagined Printer's Row.

Dearborn Renovations Associates developed Printer's Row, starting with the largest empty structure on Dearborn Street, the Transportation Building. To begin they listed goals, including concessions from City Hall to forgive back taxes, also the need to create a sufficient number of loft apartments to make the project pay. Along with the economics, the goals board also listed design elements such as abundant natural light which led to open loft-like spaces. The project took several years, but it came together and inspired others like it in the area. Another participant in the movement on Printer's Row was SOM partner Bruce Graham, who became a supporter, and later a client, of Larry's infusion of historical design in contemporary architecture.

The Transportation Building project affirmed Larry's belief that old buildings were crucial to the city. "I think we have all learned a great deal about the design of new buildings because of the attention that has been paid to old ones," he told *Architectural Record*. Larry also found a small building among the larger ones in the neighborhood, and moved his office into it with a new partner, Paul Hansen. One of Booth Hansen's first commissions was for Grace Place, another renovation in which the firm created a religious sanctuary in a Printer's Row loft.

It escaped no one's attention that historical architecture was having a general revival in this period. The critic Charles Jencks wrote *The Language of Post-Modern Architecture* in 1977 which featured the work of architects who incorporated traditional forms (arcades, domes, etc.) into otherwise modern buildings. Post-modernism's short history was fraught with controversies and critical failures, but Larry's judicious use of historical elements enabled him

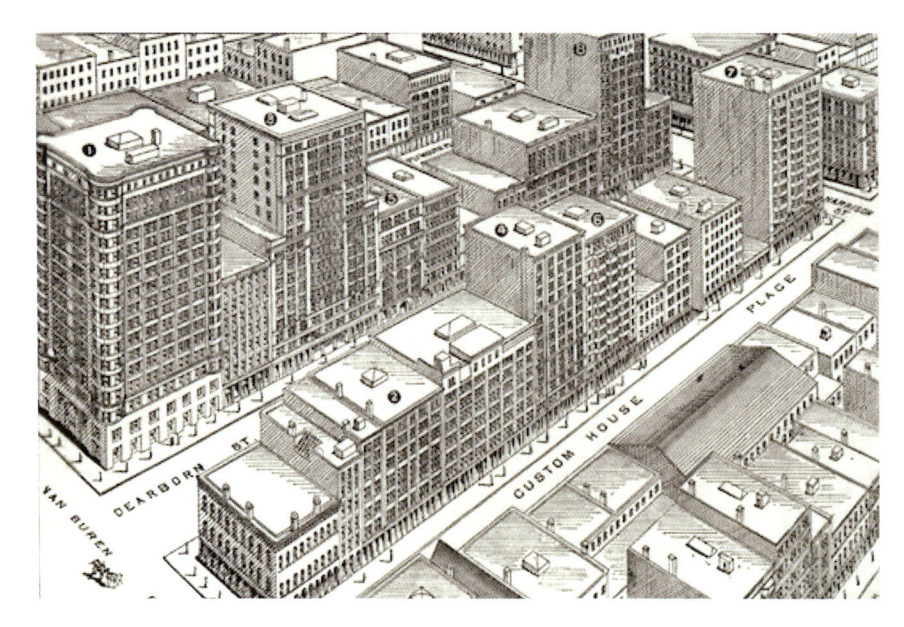

Old Printer's Row on Dearborn Street was lined with durable industrial buildings. After a period of decline, many of these buildings were well-suited to rebirth as residential lofts within walking distance of downtown Chicago.

to properly blend contemporary function with the traditional, or post-modern, gesture.

A significant success along these lines was a new home for a family on a sliver of land in Lincoln Park. What became called the House of Light was for a contractor-friend, Bert Lipman, and his wife Diane, an art historian. The process began, as always for Larry, with intense dialogue about the clients' needs. Achieving abundant natural light on the narrow lot would call for glassy transparency. Yet, the Lipmans also wanted to be harmonious neighbors on a street of mostly older buildings.

Talking with Diane Lipman, Larry learned that she wanted "to live inside a work of art." She said she was particularly interested in Renaissance art, which reinforced the idea that the house needed a traditional profile. Naturally, they began talking about Palladio, which was rare in any discussion that even touched on modernism. Yet Larry believed that Palladio's flowing spaces created effects, especially of openness and light, which made the Italian master's work sublime. These insights led to a design for the Lipmans that was symmetrical in layout and which highlighted openness. Outside it was touched by traditional detail, which created a harmonious feel on the street.

The name House of Light was inspired by an article in the *Tribune* shortly after completion. Reporter Mary Daniels praised the house for its beauty and economy, which was emphatic proof that modern spaces can be harmonious with traditional forms. For the design team at Booth Hansen it affirmed that a simple, disciplined process could lead to a result designed without preconceptions, and in a manner which was, as Larry would term it only later, "modern beyond style."

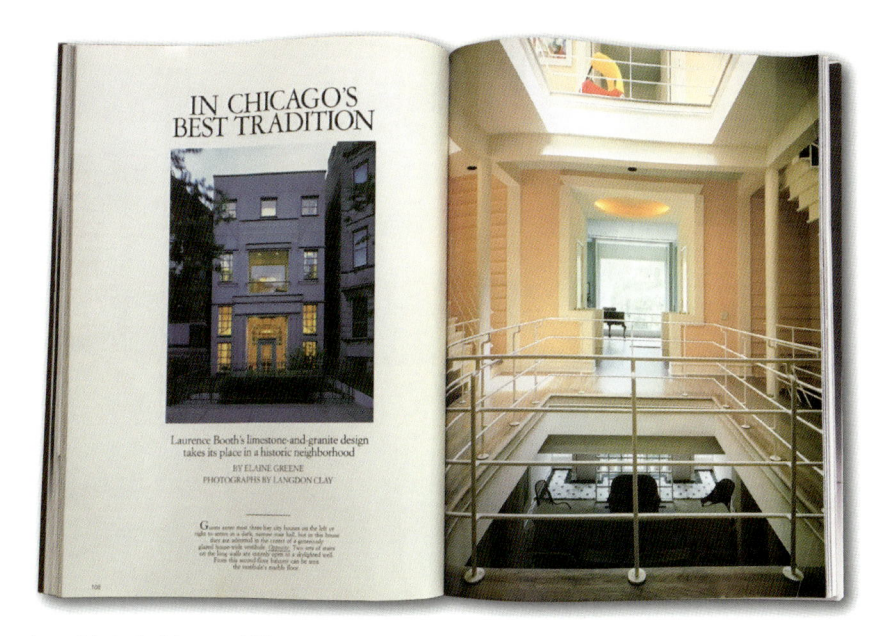

Bruce Graham.

An article in Architectural Digest

Adamson House

Lake Forest, Illinois, 1978

The Adamson House is a gracefully integrated blend of a simple series of modernist boxes, an emphatic presence in a wooded glade in the suburb, and a formal procession of interior spaces. In the same way that the Cartesian rigor of its exterior geometry highlights in counterpoint the wooded site, its Palladian order does the same within the asymmetrical plan. Each room has a function: living room, dining room, library and ultimately in this succession, an alcove for books.

Order marks the spirit of the house. Even the playfully unconventional elevations outside are proportioned with rectangular windows which balance the profile. Yellow walls which verge to ochre, and silvery green on doors and trim, have a modern sense, as do interior elements such as an open stairway and steel posts. Inside, round bulls-eye openings overhead are lined up to create a sense of connectivity—which also emphasizes separateness—and even enable a view from a second floor catwalk on one end of the house to the other, and through to the outside. Travertine, rich wood and traditional furniture (also a grand piano of the original owners) are highlighted and not hidden in the large skylighted spaces. In many ways, the design emphasizes that there is much that connects a modern house with the comforts of tradition.

Side view of the exterior (above) suggests the complex spatial divisions within the Adamson House (right).

The house opens in a variety of ways to the wooded glade of its site.

The Adamson House features rectilinear formality while promising surprising space inside.

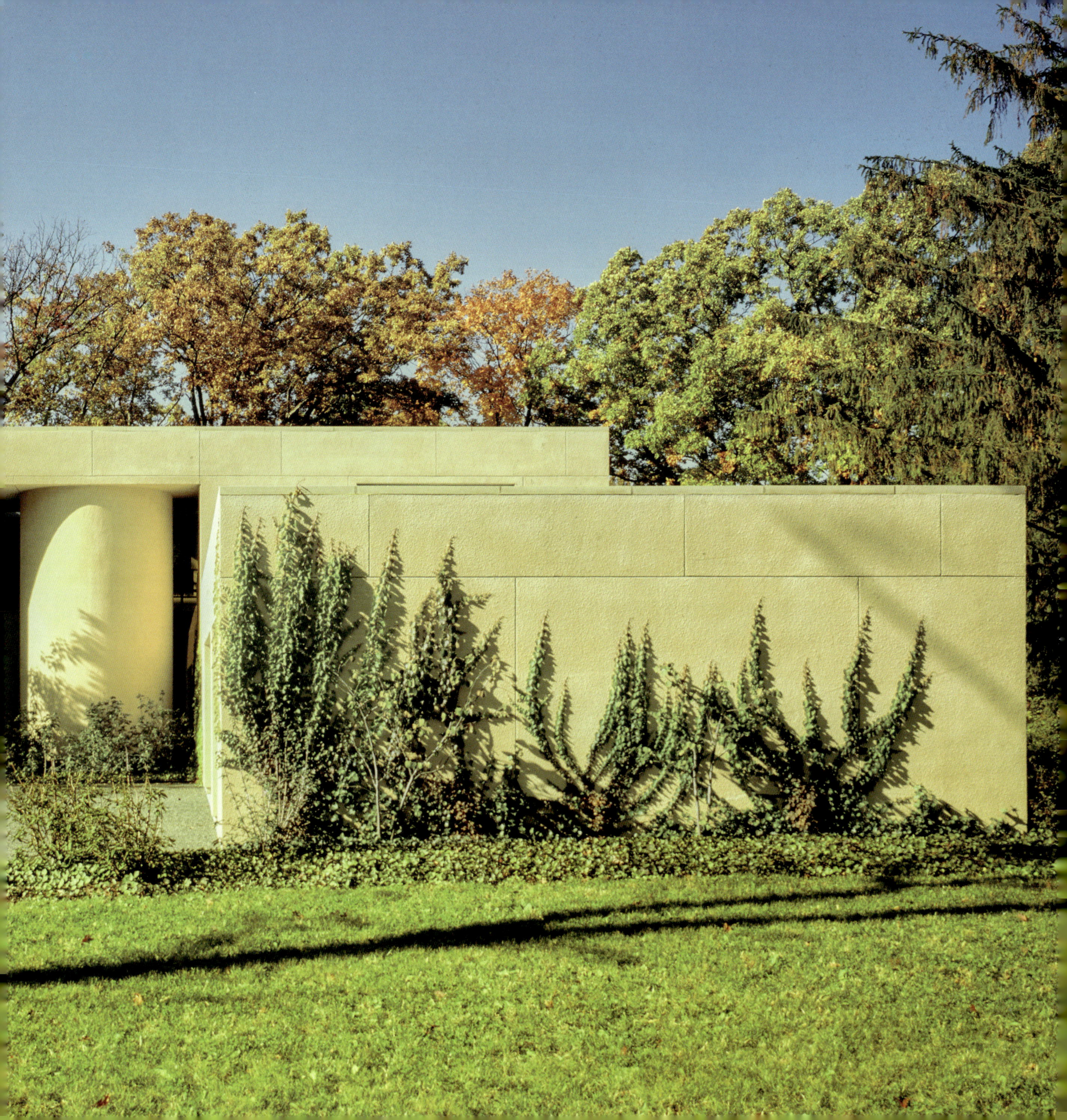

House of Light
Chicago, 1983

Booth Hansen's House of Light became a signature project for Larry Booth in the 1980s. It was also a signpost design for other architects who were eager to incorporate the warmth of tradition in otherwise modern work. This project began with an understanding of the values of the clients. Bert and Diane Lipman were clear that they wanted light and open space, certainly modern features, but also the harmony inherent in tradition.

Diane Lipman's profession as an art historian brought the Renaissance into their conversations, and invoked Larry's long familiarity with Palladio. Classical architecture had been derogated by modernism as false and imitative, but Larry's study of Palladio's 16th century Italian villas recalled the Renaissance master's skill with interlocking space and use of interpenetrating natural light.

On a narrow sight that admitted no opening on the lateral sides, the design uses a skylight, overlapping rooms and borrowed light from front and back, in an interior of symmetry and conspicuous craftsmanship.

Outside, large windows and arched transoms are attractive and functional in bringing light from the street. While straightforward, the street elevation was hardly simple to design. It required countless iterations to achieve modern transparency and traditional profile in equal measure.

This was what Chicago was waiting for in the later stages of the Miesian period, as witnessed by an article in the *Chicago Tribune* shortly after the building was complete. "It is in itself an object of art, a massive sculpture with an outside and an inside that you can walk through, a form that engages and delights the mind," the newspaper reported. The sense of space and light seemed modern. The exterior of articulated windows and carved stone appeared classical. It is not that it straddles the modern and the traditional. It is more that it is deeply settled in what made each one desirable.

The House of Light was designed for space and light in a limited standard Chicago lot size of 25 by 125 feet.

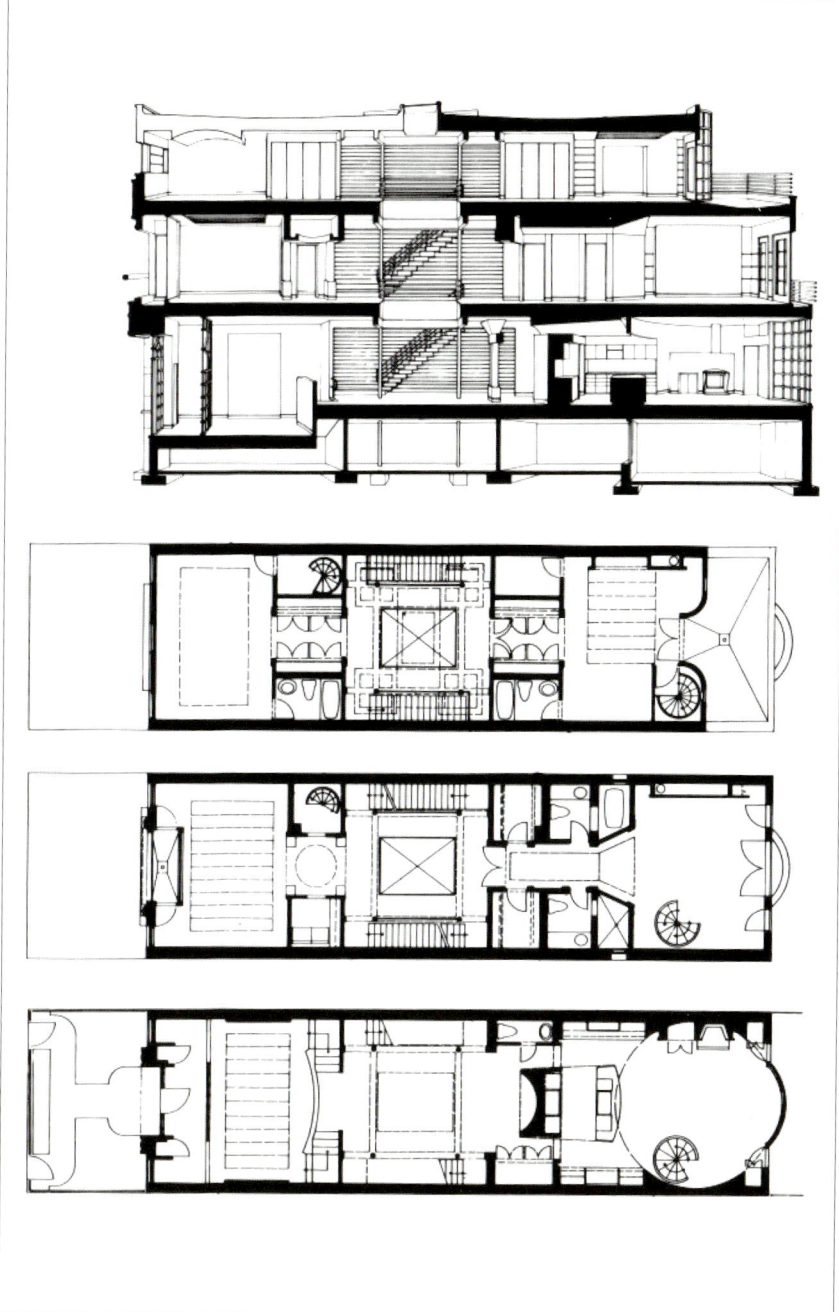

In the daytime, the house blends with its traditional neighbors. In the evening its modern character glows.

The detailing reinforces the unified space of the central atrium that reaches from first floor to skylight.

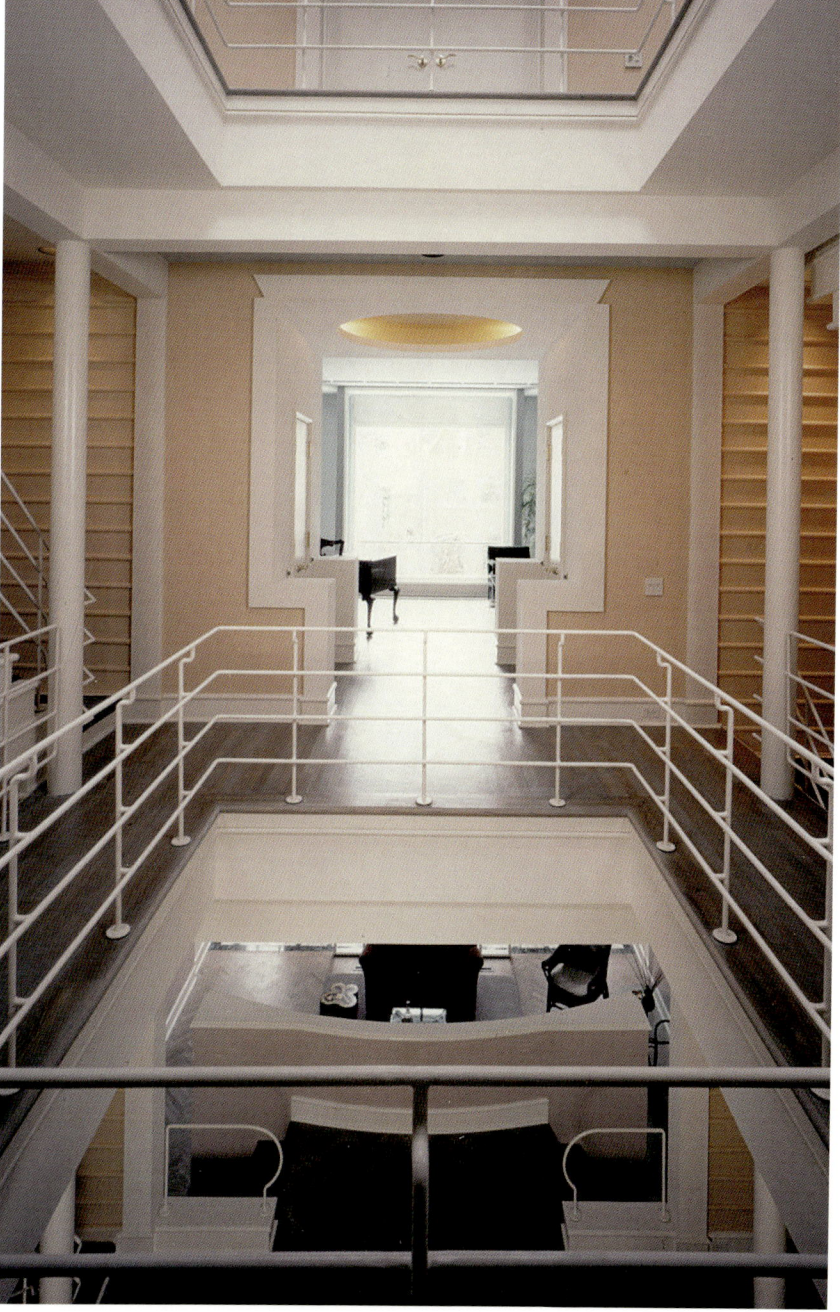

The interior is distinctly modern while the arch of the front door and interpenetrating sunlight throughout reach back to history.

Chicken Coop and Zinc House

Lake Bluff, Illinois, 1988 and 1998

A collage assembled the many elements of the simple Chicken Coop.

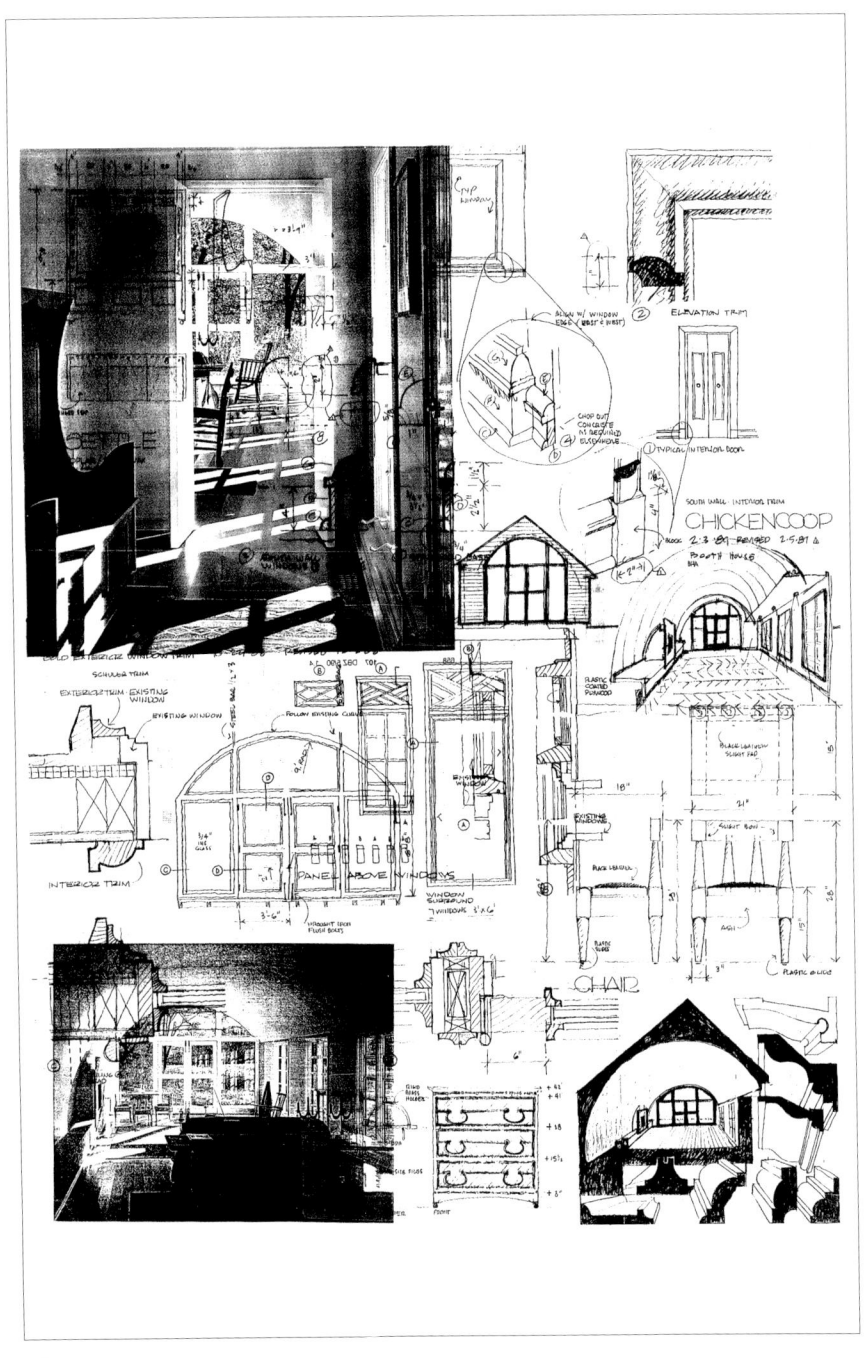

When Larry and his wife purchased several acres of land that had been vacant for decades, they found that there was more to save on the property than to build. Its oak savanna and prairie had more than 100 native species which changed the character of landscape several times every year. The only structure was what might have been an abandoned chicken coop, a long, pitched-roof building which to Larry represented "embedded energy," something to preserve.

Echoing the agricultural tone of the building was not difficult. Vertical windows on the south face are lined up to emphasize the length of the structure and even suggest (with some imagination) organized production inside. Siding is agricultural bead board, and the trim inside and out is hand-milled and easily assembled. Wide-plank floors are left unstained, and the long shotgun-style main room is punctuated with low furniture to emphasize its length. The crucial problem was to find a way to merge the spirit of prairie with that of the house. The solution was an arched ceiling which terminates at a glass wall, providing a full view of the wild. It transforms the feel of the interior to something of delicate spring or fiery autumn as the colorful plant life reflects its seasons.

In 2009, the Chicken Coop was joined by a larger house that would become a main residence for the extended Booth family. The Zinc House is massed like a barn, features large openings, also like a true barn, and has subsidiary wings added as needed. Zinc cladding, which promises to be maintenance free for a half century at least, and the pitched metal roofs do nothing to spoil the agricultural effect. And its dark color allows featured elements of the place, gardens and prairie, to enjoy their highlighted role year-round.

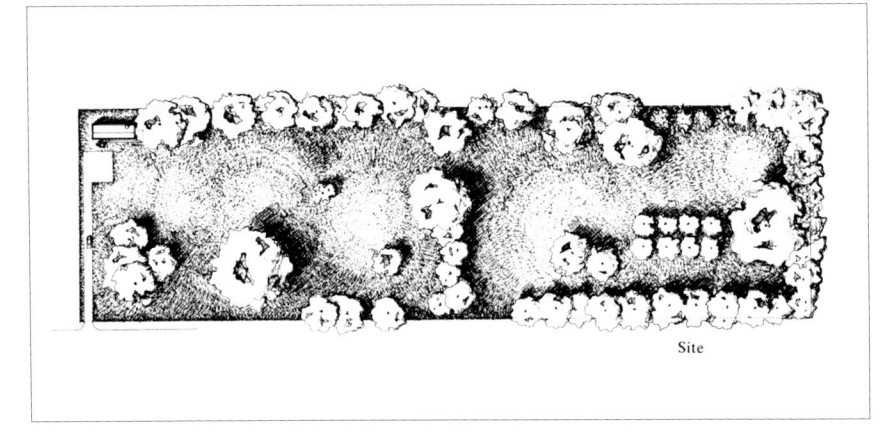

Site

The original structure featured attractive proportions which were domesticated with an arched ceiling, detailed windows on the side and generous opening to an ever-changing prairie.

51

The spirit of the farm is present in the Zinc House with a trellis and functional additions.

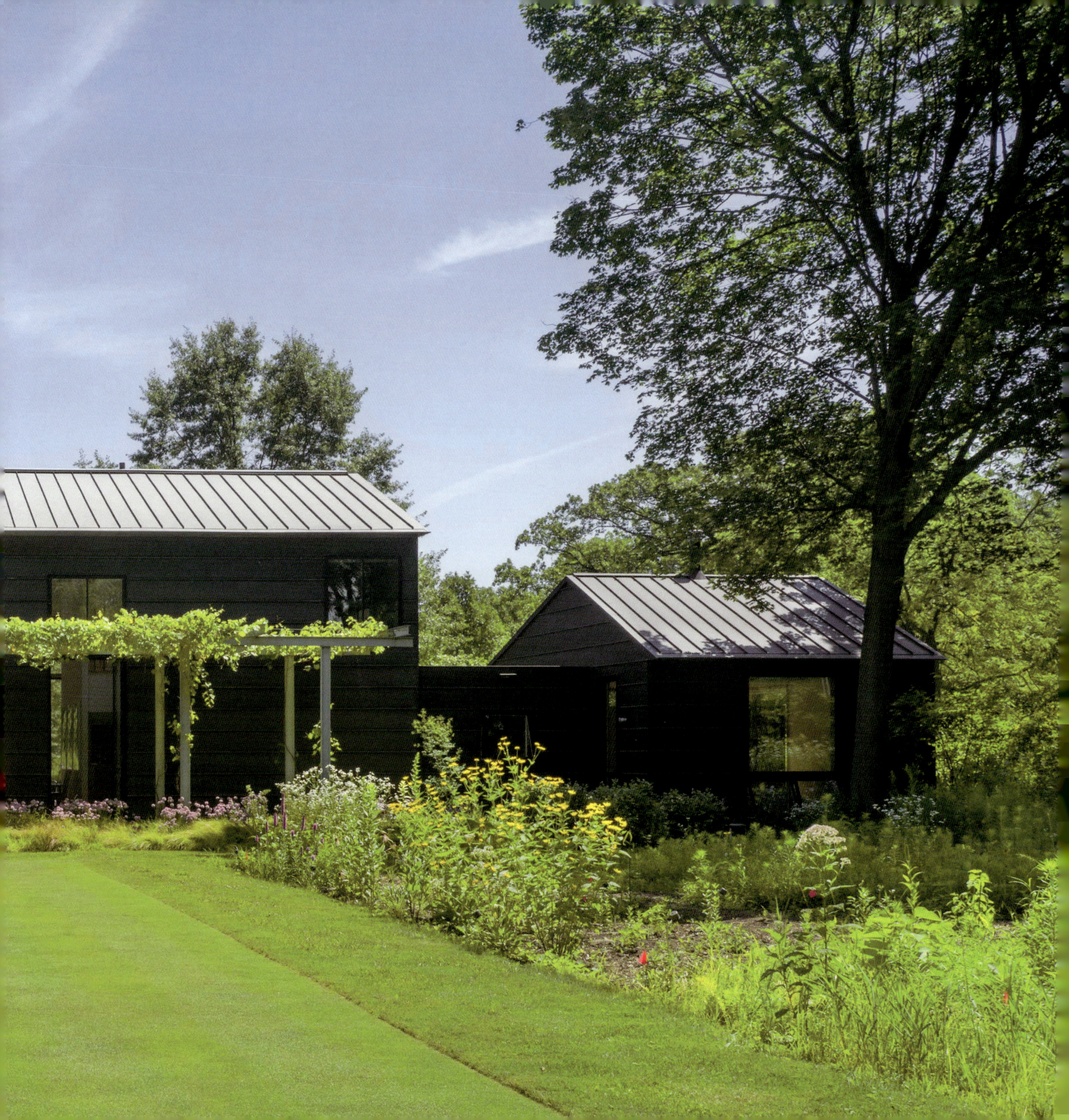

The beauty of nature is primary in the design.

The structure is a simple box. Complexity is created with an enfilade floor plan.

Memorable furniture is of simple form and handmade in modest maple.

This page and opposite: Simple geometry in architecture and furnishings provide a counterpoint to the rich and ever-changing character of the natural world outside.

57

Grace Place Episcopal
Chicago, 1989

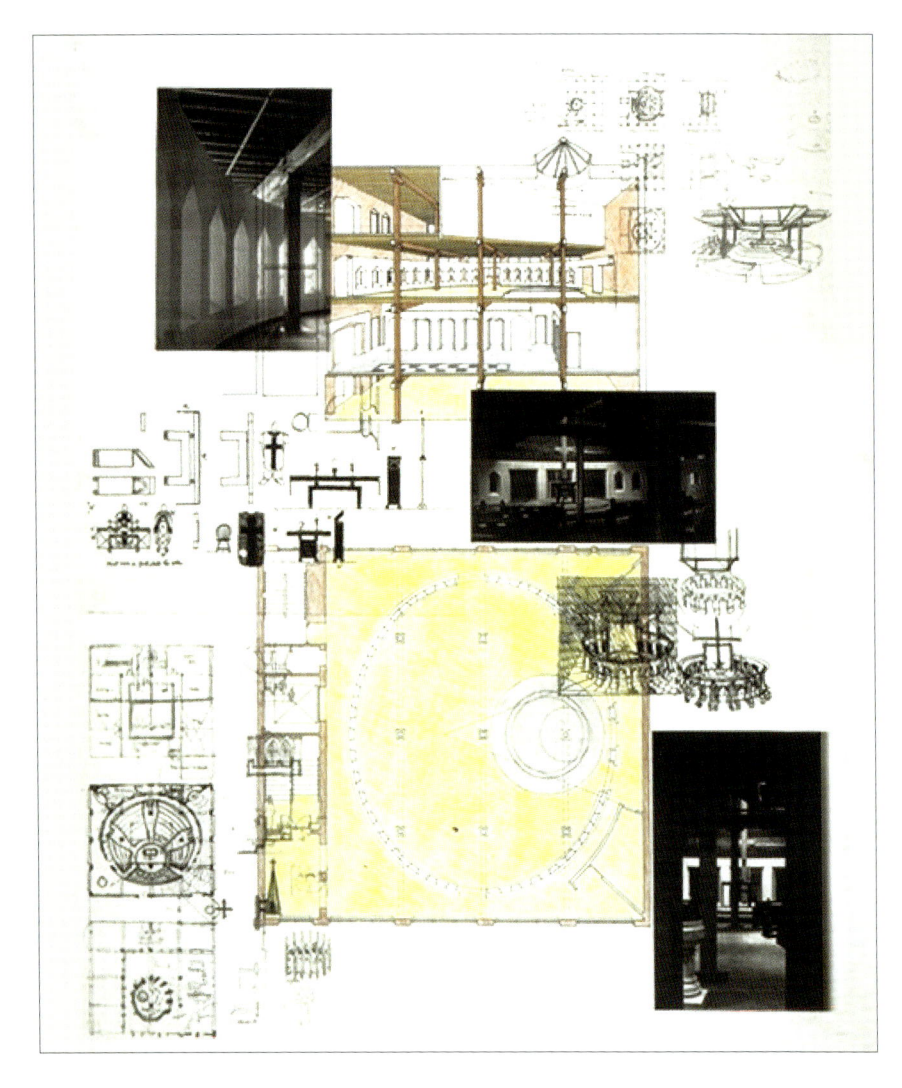

The design of Grace Place harmoniously blends disparate elements.

As downtown Chicago began its revitalization in the 1980s, the Printer's Row community, on the Near South Side, and Grace Episcopal Church, a congregation which has existed since the 1840s, were drawn to each other. The church had been in the South Loop and needed a new location. Printer's Row was burgeoning but needed institutions. Effecting the marriage became partly an architectural problem.

As Larry was designing early loft apartments in the neighborhood, he met with Grace Episcopal's Rev. Bill Casady to discuss what was possible. They visited the three-story brick building that the church had eyed, and Casady wondered if the heavy beams and brick walls were dignified enough. Larry reminded the pastor of a passage from scripture: "Wherever you are gathered in my name, I am there with you."

From that point, the process was straightforward. The printer's loft was designed originally for flexibility. A circular sanctuary for 100 or so people was created with a cylindrical wall pierced with Gothic arches, filtering light from the large windows of the building's perimeter. Cut from the ceiling a skylight brings light through the beam work to the altar. Perhaps most fortuitously, a T-joint in the hewn-timber structure behind the altar is highlighted with an industrial fish plate, a conspicuous high-tech crucifix.

As the project was designed in a period of post-modern freedom, the liturgical furniture and benches could be marked with suggestions of the ecclesiastical without attempting to create a traditional church. In fact, Casady decided to rename the church Grace Place and label it not a "church," rather a "worship center." This would avoid a legal clash with an old neighborhood bar, prohibited from serving liquor next door to a church. The nomenclature also encouraged the church to open the sanctuary to other denominations, a gesture both economical for the congregation and ecumenical, both values being consonant with the spirit of the Printer's Row community.

The altar has a crucifix-like metal plate which is part of the structure.

Light was a prime objective in the loft's original design. Natural illumination penetrates through a ceiling which opens to a skylight, and through lancet openings in the oval wall that defines the worship space.

Nothing is done to disguise the industrial origins of the building nor its modern ecclesiastical use.

Navy Pier
Redevelopment Proposal, Chicago, 1989

Booth Hansen's approach to the redevelopment of Navy Pier involved a limited palette for such a large project—of brick similar to that used in the 1916 original, glass and steel to construct the diversity of spaces for tourism, restaurants, theaters and events requiring significant open space.

The choice of materials would preserve the historic character of the pier which was built originally in a style that fused Georgian design with early-modern streamlining. The glass and steel shed-like structures would provide long-span interiors for many proposed functions while also emphasizing the spirit of a true maritime pier which extends more than 3,000 feet out into Lake Michigan.

By employing metal frames, the Navy Pier project created a series of vast interior spaces with a technology that reaches back to the early use of glass and steel.

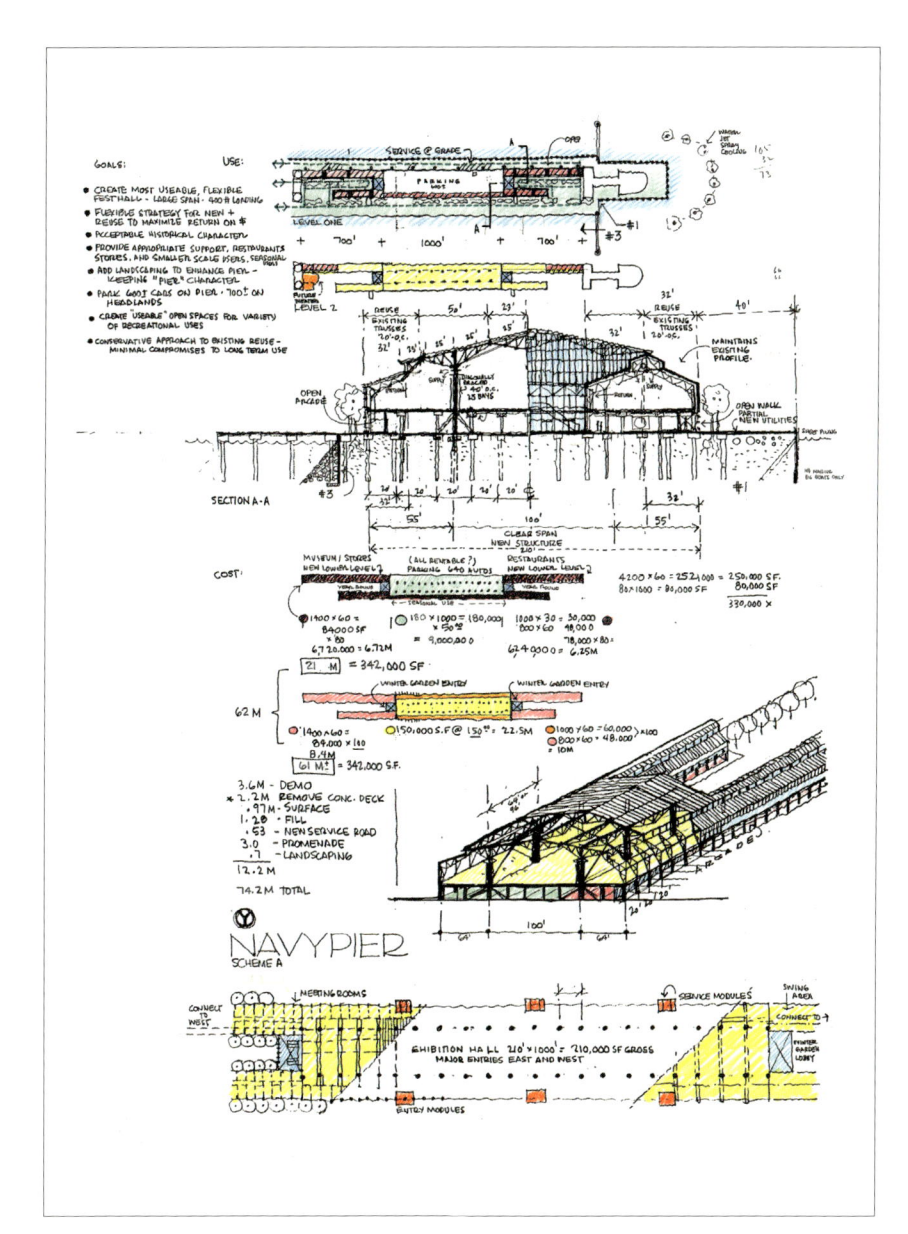

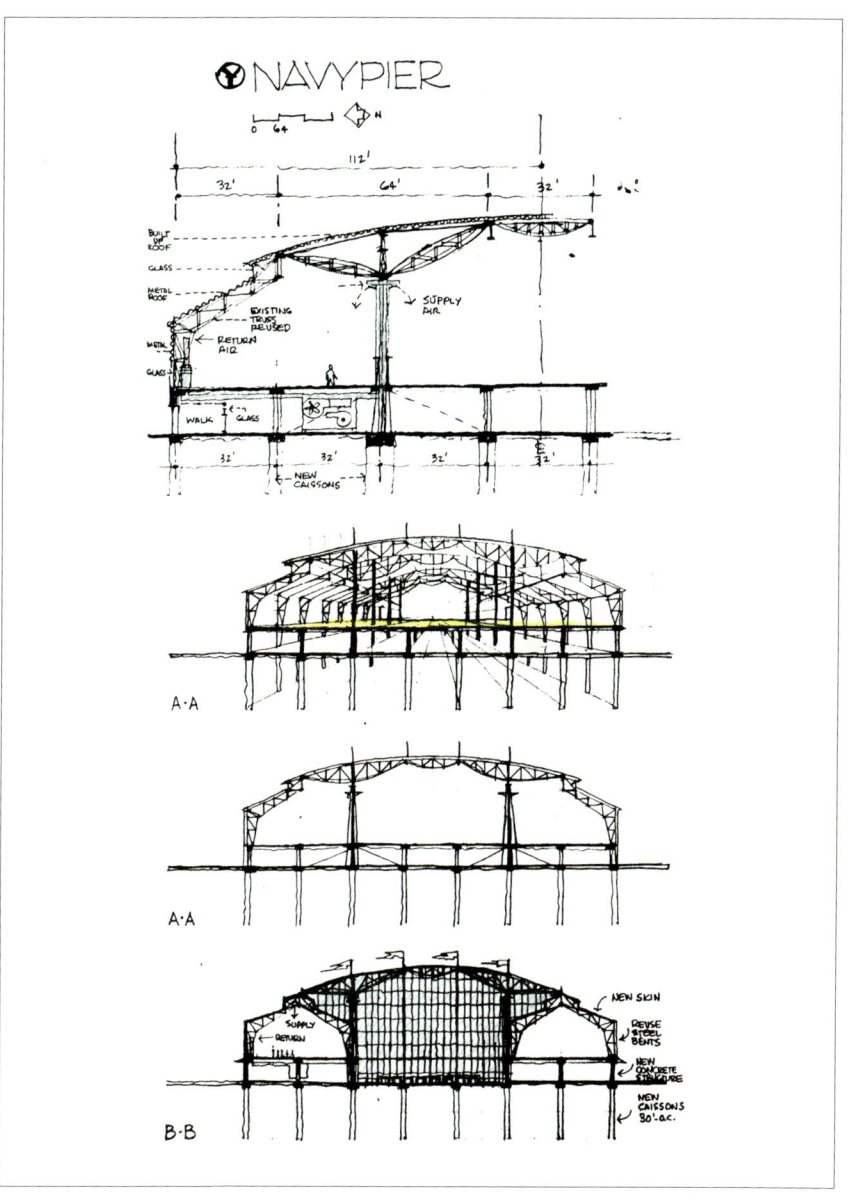

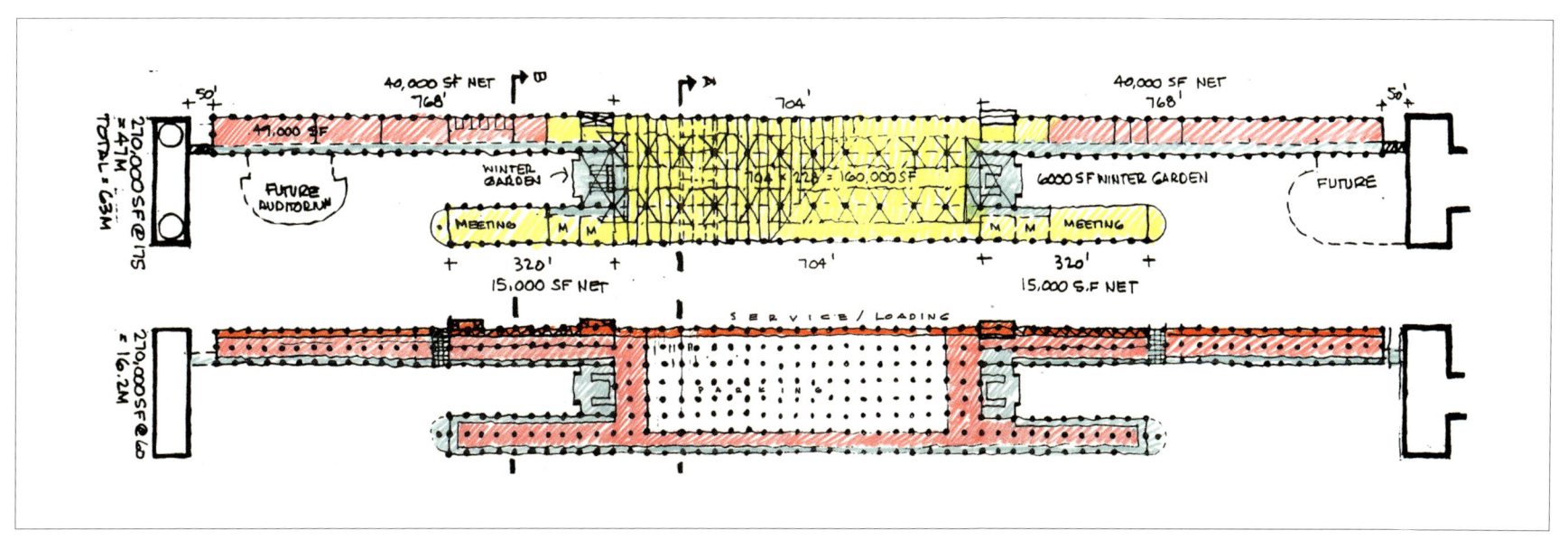

NAVY PIER

Kinkead Pavilion

of the Krannert Museum
University of Illinois-Urbana, 1990

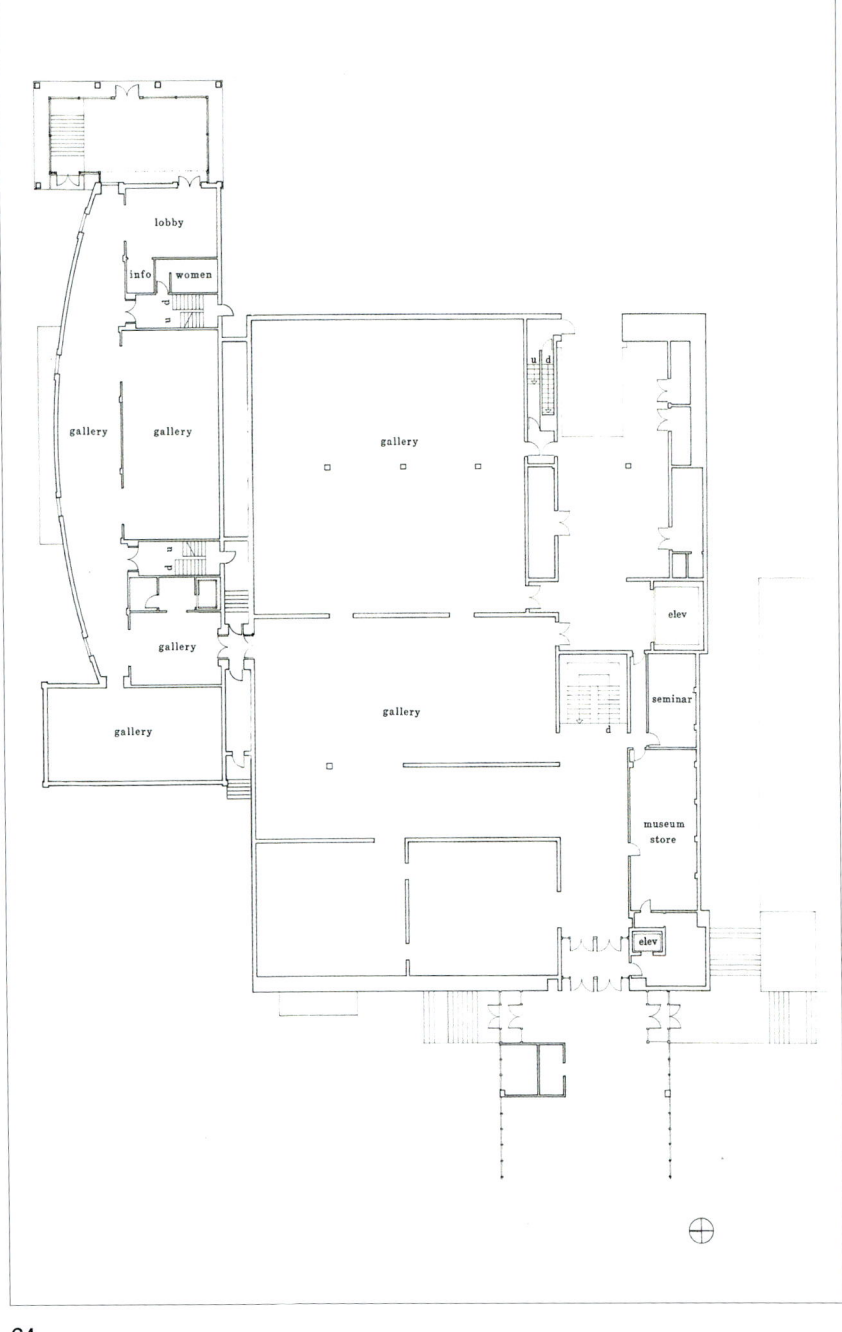

Larry's view of architectural history, and of post-modernism in the late 20th century, included his conviction that many design problems had been solved in the past, and that modern architects are correct to use them. This he did in the Kinkead Pavilion of the Krannert Museum at the University of Illinois-Urbana. The objectives of the building's program were not overtly historic. For one, the existing museum had two floors of exhibit space not connected to one another in a graceful manner. A secondary need was that the renewed Krannert would help reestablish a cross axis of the university campus, which had been compromised over recent decades and building projects.

The Kinkead Pavilion achieves both with a set of solutions that were in some ways counterintuitive. The main entry is given not to the long side of the building, but to the short end. This is a double-high volume wrapped in glass. (Glass on the long side would be unsuitable for needed gallery space.) The entry has a modern staircase which links the two floors. Outside, the three-sided portico, with grand columns, is aligned with the long-neglected cross-axis of the campus which now passes through the portico and toward the main quadrangle.

As if the building anticipated the short life of post-modernism, the columns and capitals are abstract, structural and well-proportioned. At the same time, the portico renders importance to the new space inside and harmonizes with the long side of the buildings, an Adamesque-inspired wall on the edge of a sculpture garden. A professor who taught in the building praised the design as an imaginative use of classicism, breaking old rules to achieve modern objectives.

The Kinkead Pavilion was designed to improve the circulation within the existing museum, also to reassert the classical plan of the century-old campus.

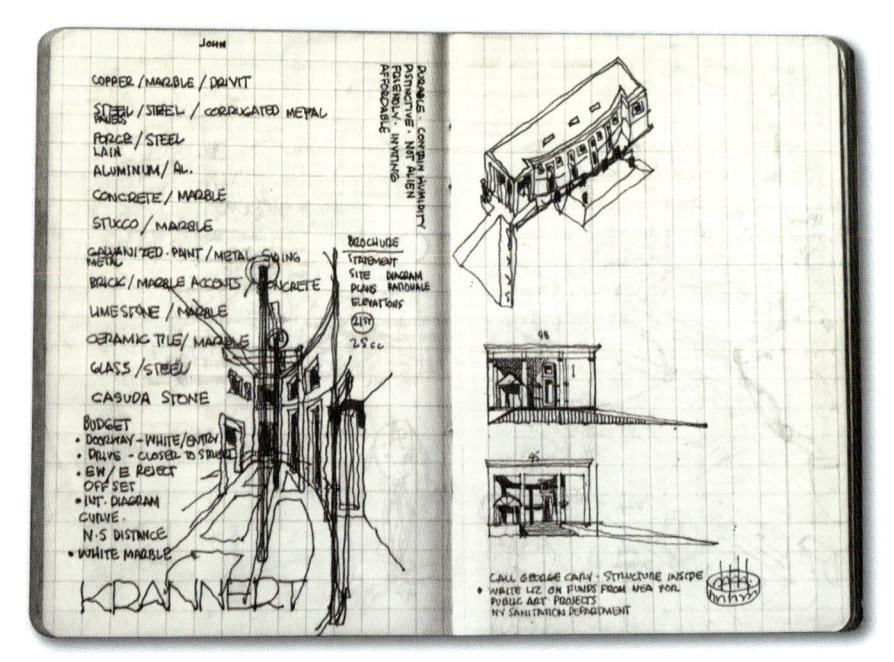

The classical gestures of the pavilion recall the spendors of the old campus.

The curved space is adjacent to the museum's older two-story structure.

Larry sketching in the Sistine Chapel.

Spirit
Forging the Invisible

Excessive architectural debate in the 1990s, Larry came to believe, was not advancing the cause of architecture at all. "One might observe an inverse proportion between the quantity of written material and the quality of the buildings," he wrote in an article entitled "An Architecture of the American Spirit" which was published in *Chicago History* magazine.

In fact, Larry continued to do his own writing and publish his ideas, but he remained the contrarian. "I can tell Architecture when I see it," he quoted a fictitious observer in this article. "It's a building with windows either too big or too small."

Larry continued to get the size of his windows about right by adhering to the design process that he had championed for more than a decade. That approach included close interaction with the client, who would know a bad window when he or she saw it, and the collaboration of colleagues, so that someone could call out any distortions which had become all too common in modernism, post-modernism, deconstructionism and other movements.

What was obvious to Larry, and strangely absent in recent architectural thinking, was that architecture is a language that has evolved over millennia. The Greeks and then the Romans established traditions that have stood the test of time. Then there was Brunelleschi, who studied the Romans in excruciating detail, and Palladio whose villas reached to the past and set examples about light and space for centuries to come. The list goes on.

Larry insisted that history was what made architecture rich with symbolism and meaning, and hardly anyplace was richer than Chicago. Sullivan evoked timeless force, praised as unprecedented by his colleagues at the time, in the sublime harmonies of his arches, columns and ornament, hardly unconnected to the past. "The vital purpose and significance of Art is that of attaining [nature's] rhythmic song," wrote Sullivan as quoted in Larry's article on the American spirit.

Larry's experience at mid-career had proved to him that spirit and even poetry represented architecture's true goal, and in recent architecture, it was rarely found in puzzles of glass, steel and air conditioning. The spirit of a building was in its feeling. And the richness of feeling depended upon the layering of memory and emotion handed down in traditional forms. In one Booth project, a rural spirit was transmitted with barn-like lines and striking views of nature. In another, religious significance was triggered by ancient iconography redrawn with modern clarity.

As Larry wrote about the ideas behind his work, it elevated his reputation, not least with clients or potential clients. It would take time, however, for these ideas to filter broadly into the profession.

Architecture at large was locked in the same battle that had raged ten years before, with the modernists who believed that technology could solve every architectural problem. As for post-modernists, they were no gentler—as the movement adorned the top of one skyscraper with a Chippendale pediment (Philip Johnson's AT&T Building), and in many other buildings with Gothic detail but without Gothic spirit.

Nevertheless, Larry went his own way, and Booth Hansen's practice grew with clients who understood that the firm's focus on spirit produced results different from the so-called styles that people were arguing about. Some elements of his work could be classical, others of it minimal, but Larry always worked to harmonize them with poetic intent. While his objective of recognizing tradition in architecture was hardly unique, Larry hit the target consistently.

Success was measured in part by the frequency with which his work was published—as if the public was hungry for architecture that touched the spirit. And as critics acknowledged the profession's overall lack of creativity in these years, Larry was joined by a few others who wanted very much to turn the corner. In the 1980s, for example, three Chicago architects founded a new press and published a facsimile edition of a 19th century portfolio of the work of Karl Schinkel. A leading architect to the Prussian court, Schinkel adapted Greek forms to buildings that were functional to the growing bureaucracy and commercial life in Berlin. His buildings were large and complex, but also stately, and they evoked pride.

Publication of the drawings inspired Larry to have a look at what inspired Schinkel, who died in 1841, and to write a *Play in Seven Scenes* about the German which appeared in the *Inland Architect* (along with an article about the portfolio). In one scene, Schinkel is at the deathbed of his mentor, and promises to continue to design with "idealism and humanism." In another, the Kaiser, who is a client and regarded as a true humanist, tells Schinkel to design a building in a purely classical form. The architect demurs. "Prussia must keep up with improvements," he says, implying that functional form does not need clash with classicism. The last scene is in the 1980s, and a student laments the modernist style he had been taught in school. Schinkel's buildings "are really beautifully made and seem to fit so well into their sites," the student says. "Perhaps we can learn something from his work."

Larry's six-act play about Karl Schinkel appeared in the Inland Architect.

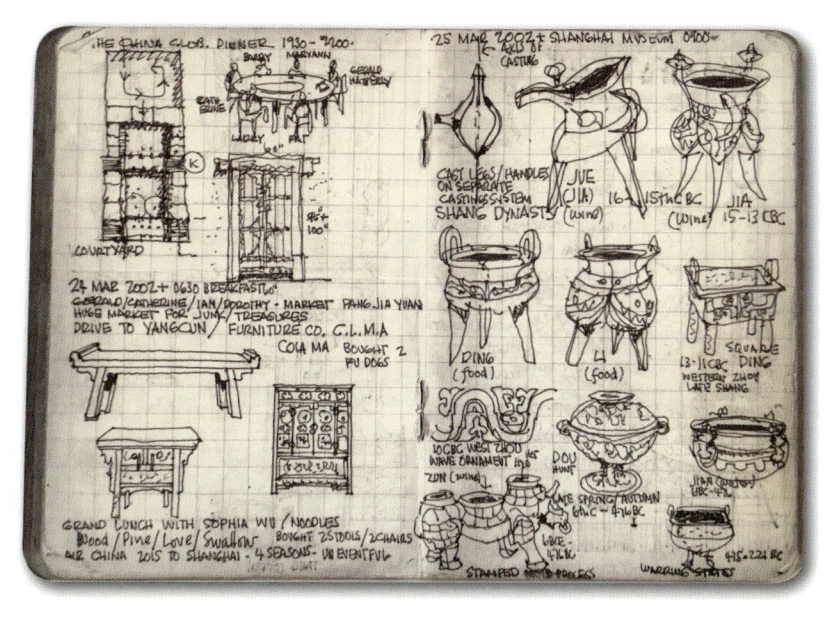

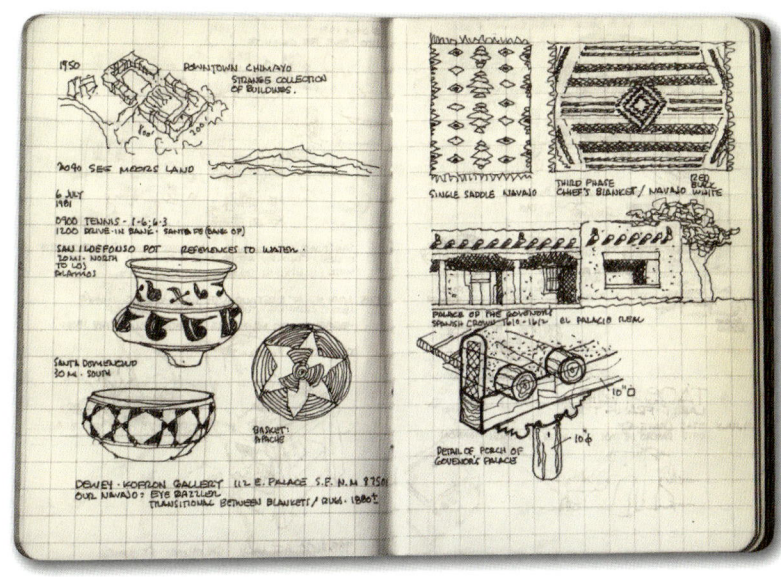

Learning from the past was entirely behind Booth Hansen's Shoreacres clubhouse in Lake Bluff. This firm was commissioned to replace a cherished building, designed by David Adler in 1923, which was destroyed in a fire. The task was to recreate the former building's feel, its spirit of domesticity, while also creating interior spaces more suitable to a modern club. This meant understanding Adler well enough to alter the original design with Adler's self-same spirit.

What made Adler exemplary was his ability to adapt historic detail—rooflines, proportion, detail—to the needs of his client. Larry's clients were different, but the lesson held true, especially as he and his team were guided, as Adler had been, by the Colonial spirit that was the original's model. Adler's eye for detail was exceptional. Larry was duly inspired not to reproduce the old objectively, rather to trust the eye in adapting it.

Larry called it "gentle synthesis," a subjective idea but indispensable to the disciplined process that was being practiced in his office. It recognized traditional templates, but also encouraged creatively distilling and assembling them. In the late years of the 20th century, Booth Hansen showed in many ways how its original and influential work was achieved, not least with refined details that infused structures with ineffable spirit.

Top: In the ancient Chinese bronze gallery of the Shanghai Museum, Larry found objects that were elaborately beautiful and absolutely functional. He was naturally motivated to save the memory in his notebook.

Middle: Larry sought visual connections between decorative design in the early American Southwest and its construction techniques.

Bottom: The Moscow subway and the circus.

Shoreacres

Lake Bluff, Illinois, 1983

The Shoreacres clubhouse recreates the spirit of a David Adler-designed building that burned to the ground in the early 1980s. The most important objective of the members charged with rebuilding the club was to have it designed with the historic charm of Adler's 1923 building, which had been inspired by an 18th century Piedmont Virginia mansion. Adler's skill was to design with proportions and details evoking the past, also to meet the actual needs of a patrician early 20th century golf club. Larry Booth's objective was to interpret both of those, and to make the building modern in the late 20th century.

Clearly, the facade is a reproduction of the style refined by landed aristocracy in old Virginia. But Larry rearranged the interior to open a transverse corridor and more spacious rooms for events that are now larger than they were when the club was founded 60 years before with 47 members. The design challenge was to provide details that transmitted the character of the old but were appropriate to the enlarged new.

Larry and his staff designed Colonial moldings and details suitable to the larger spaces, such as a trophy cabinet for a new lounge, and a pedimented overmantel fused to the cornice moldings. Interlocking interiors now provide spaciousness, suitable for larger club events. Texture, color and the use of varied materials also help delineate more intimate "rooms" while not walling them off from larger spaces. Painted wallpaper appears in a reception room, and wainscoting which helps define spaces is used more liberally than it was in the original club.

Floor-to-ceiling sash windows create bays that open the interior to the outside bluff and Lake Michigan. These are larger than those of the past, but they are executed with patterns and rhythm extrapolated from old Adler plans and those of Piedmont plantations. Shoreacres demonstrates that details can transmit tradition while skillful use of space renders a work of architecture timeless.

Precise proportion are central in David Adler's classic design. Booth Hansen architects achieved the spirit of the original through drawing and iteration.

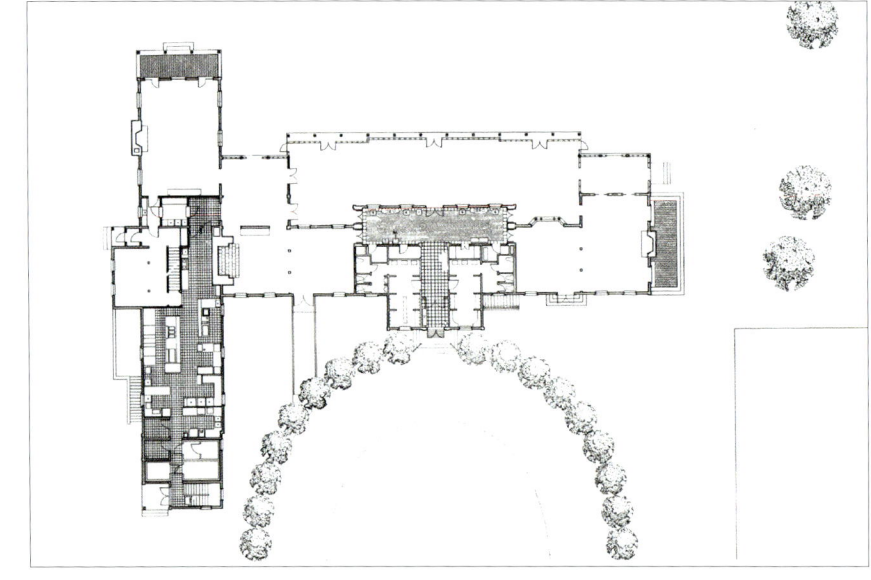

The rear of the building features a modernity which Adler's original only suggested.

71

The interiors of Shoreacres provide open spaces required by the modern club. It retains warmth through detailing inspired by Adler's original plans.

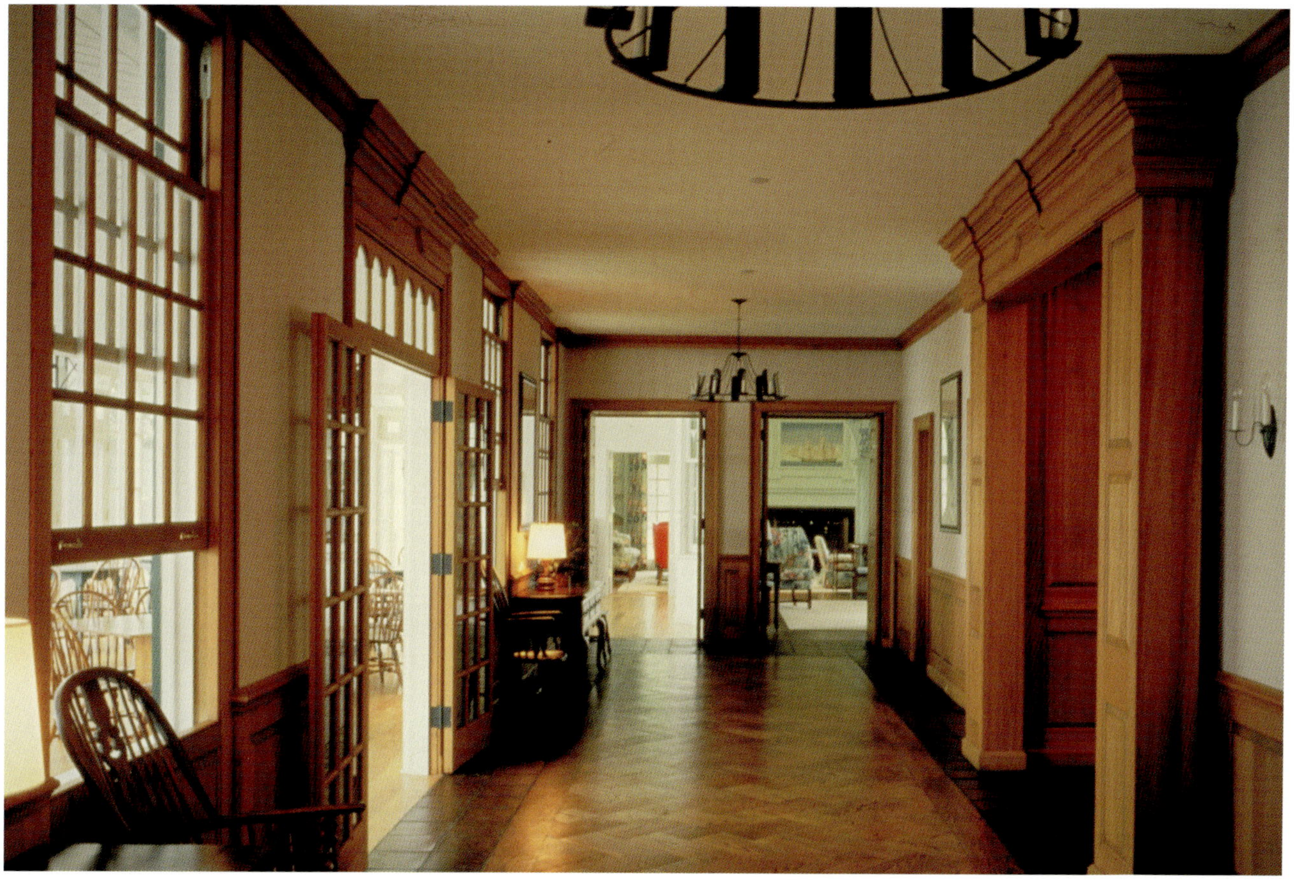

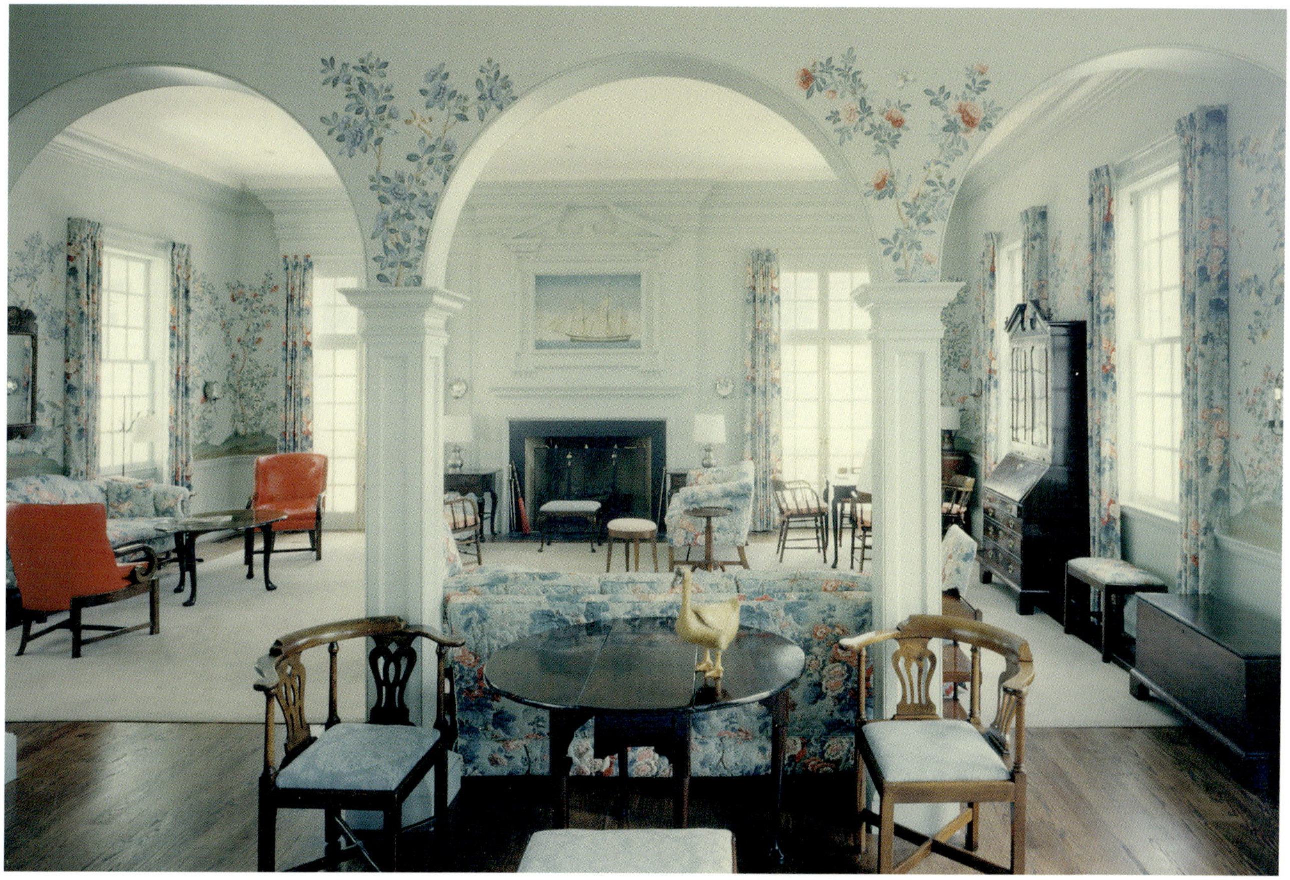

Dunes Club

New Buffalo, Michigan, 1989

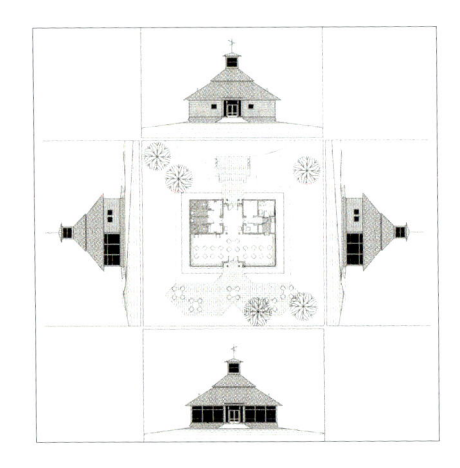

The clubhouse of the Dunes Club in Michigan is inconspicuous at first glance, as is the nine-hole golf course that runs along a sandy section of Lake Michigan's eastern shore. Yet the course has acquired an international following for its subtle terrain and world-class design. Likewise, this small structure provides a range of sensations larger than its size. It is divided between a tiny locker room where the organization of its cubby-holed changing room is zen-like in its modesty, and one side of the interior opens to a small terrace. Sited on a high point on the 90-acre property, the clubhouse provides views that unfold to the eye, as if in layers.

The architecture is utilitarian in profile, though its unique effects are highlighted slightly by a double roof reminiscent of a Japanese teahouse, the simplicity of which appears to have inspired the delicate construction inside and out. A rectangular cupola overhead affirms that this is America, as this light-giving detail recalls a Colonial manse or Midwestern barn. These many notes are unified into a building as uncomplicated as it is unique.

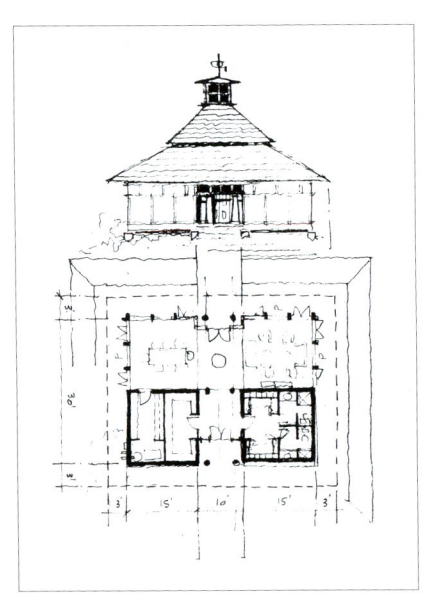

The club is equipped for modern function in a small historically inspired structure.

The interior is rustic, but its simplicity and abundant natural light from the rear windows are timeless.

75

Schuler House
Lake Bluff, Illinois, 1989

Openness and light are provided in a large home of intimate spaces throughout.

When the Schuler House was being designed, the Booth Hansen process already involved the client's detailed list of requirements and needs. With Mr. Schuler the interview verged into the subjective, as Larry asked him about how he wanted to "feel" in the various part of the future house that they discussed. The result of these conversations led to a home that has flowing modern space, but also the intimacy wrought of milled detail, traditional molding and columns which define but do not wall off space.

Other elements of the house were driven not by style, rather by specific desires of the client. The views on the bluff and light from Lake Michigan were important, and this suggested tall elevations and large east-facing windows. As the trees of the site are mature, the skyward reach of the house inspired gables and even a tower over the roof, rendered with the picturesqueness of modest Queen Anne cottages. Materials are durable, thus sustainable, including the quarried limestone masonry. Sections of zinc cladding reinforce the sustainability idea and gives it a modern note that does not clash with the traditional feel.

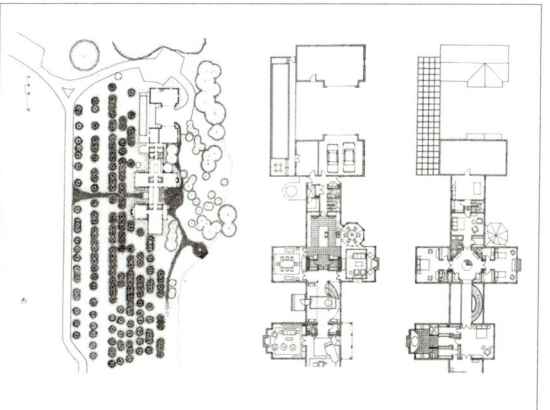

The Schuler House is a sprawling structure unified by careful organization.

77

Motorola Museum of Electronics

Schaumburg, Illinois, 1990

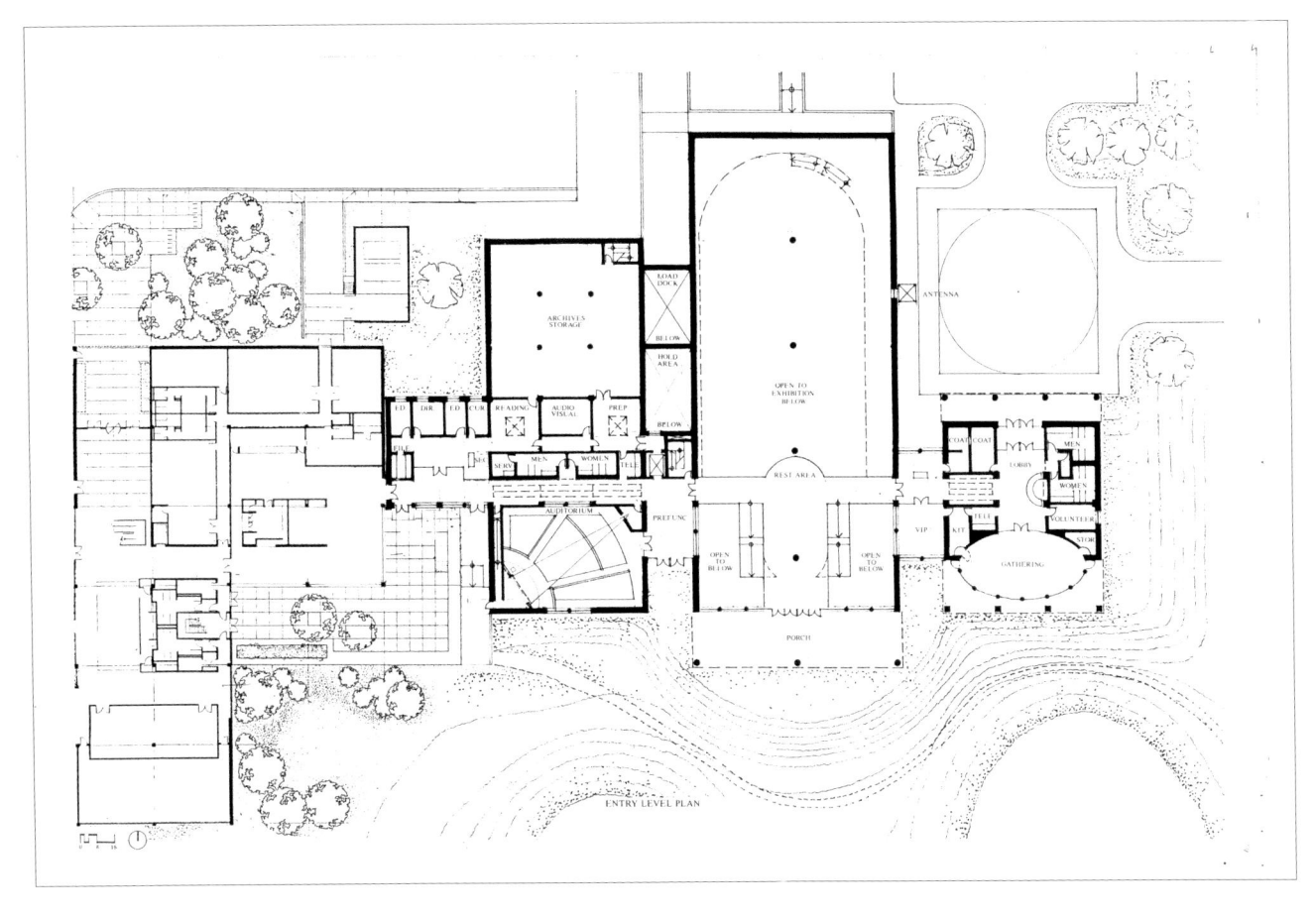

The museum's siting on the edge of a wetland.

The *parti* of the Motorola Museum was invented after the client, the chairman of the major electronics corporation, told Larry that he had been at a trade event in Europe where he walked in an entry above the main floor and could see the entire show at once. This suggestion led to a large open exhibition space, 100 by 250 feet, and the main entry at balcony level with a panoramic view of the whole.

One challenge of the design required an invisible solution. For the below-grade exhibition space, a foundation was engineered to withstand the pressure and humidity of a flood plain all around the site. In an overall economical design, the open truss work of arched I-beams, which recall Belle Époque exhibition halls, are expressed also on the exterior by giant vaults which can be seen from the Interstate that runs past the Motorola campus. Exterior walls are wrought of careful brickwork, a Flemish bond with projecting headers in some sections, which is visible on close inspection.

Inside, the immense modern space with its spirit of the past is appropriate for Motorola's story which reaches to the early part of the 20th century (it invented the car radio) and became a key participant in 21st century telecommunications (as an early manufacturer of cell phones). Thus the building is harmonious with the story of a company that has enjoyed prosperity for a significant portion of American history.

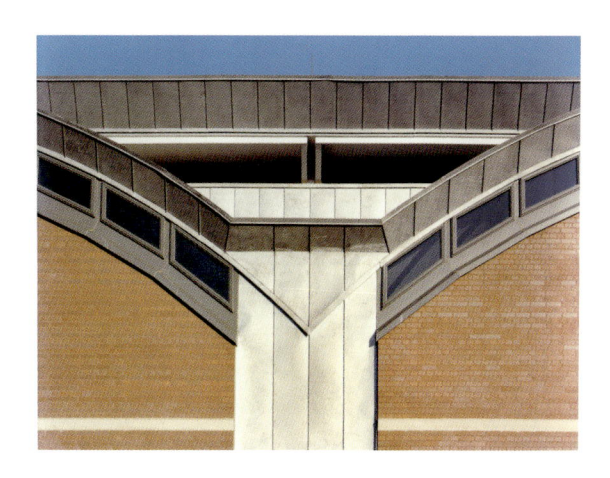

For a museum of a vast open interior, barrel arches reminiscent of Roman baths are employed along with the craftsmanship that one expects from this client, a leading maker of electronics.

From the entry, visitors would arrive at a balcony with a full view of exhibits below.

Some exhibits are historic, others futuristic. The architecture has classic touches that enclose an up-to-date space.

Benninghoven House
Chicago, 1995

"I was forever thinking, what can I do to make it lighter, simpler?" Larry said about designing the Benninghoven House on a narrow lot in Lincoln Park, Chicago, with mostly traditional houses as neighbors. His charge was to create a new home, appropriate to the streetscape, with abundant space and light inside, and which would contain only the most essential furnishings and ornament.

Some essential items brought to the design by the client were quite specific though wildly varied, such as a Corbusier sofa, a collection of primitive antique toys, plus some simple Shaker-like tables and cabinets. Being designed after the success of Booth Hansen's House of Light, this commission was a further exercise in blending the minimalism of modernity with the warmth of something traditional and in this case intensely personal.

Openness was a given. To accompany it would be exquisite craftsmanship, such as the spindled rail of the second floor balcony that wraps around a central atrium. The millwork is very fine, including a stairway that appears on second glance to defy gravity. Partial walls enhance the sense of open space and the effect of shared light. Wide plank flooring and folk-art rugs affirm the rusticity of the place.

The Benninghoven House is an example of creating a unique character or spirit on a work of architecture by careful synthesis of so-called styles. It is particularly true, if not obvious, outside on the facade, which is designed with a symmetrical geometry of large windows, trimmed lightly with limestone. Its harmony with the rest of the neighborhood was the result of countless iterations of drawing before it appeared natural, timeless. Larry mentioned Mondrian in describing it, not so much because of the way it looks, but because of the care and precision of the exceedingly simple elements.

The house occupies a site of standard urban width and depth.

Simplicity marks the interior which has the spaciousness of the modern and the craftsmanship of the past.

Old St. Patrick's Church

Renovation, Chicago, 1997

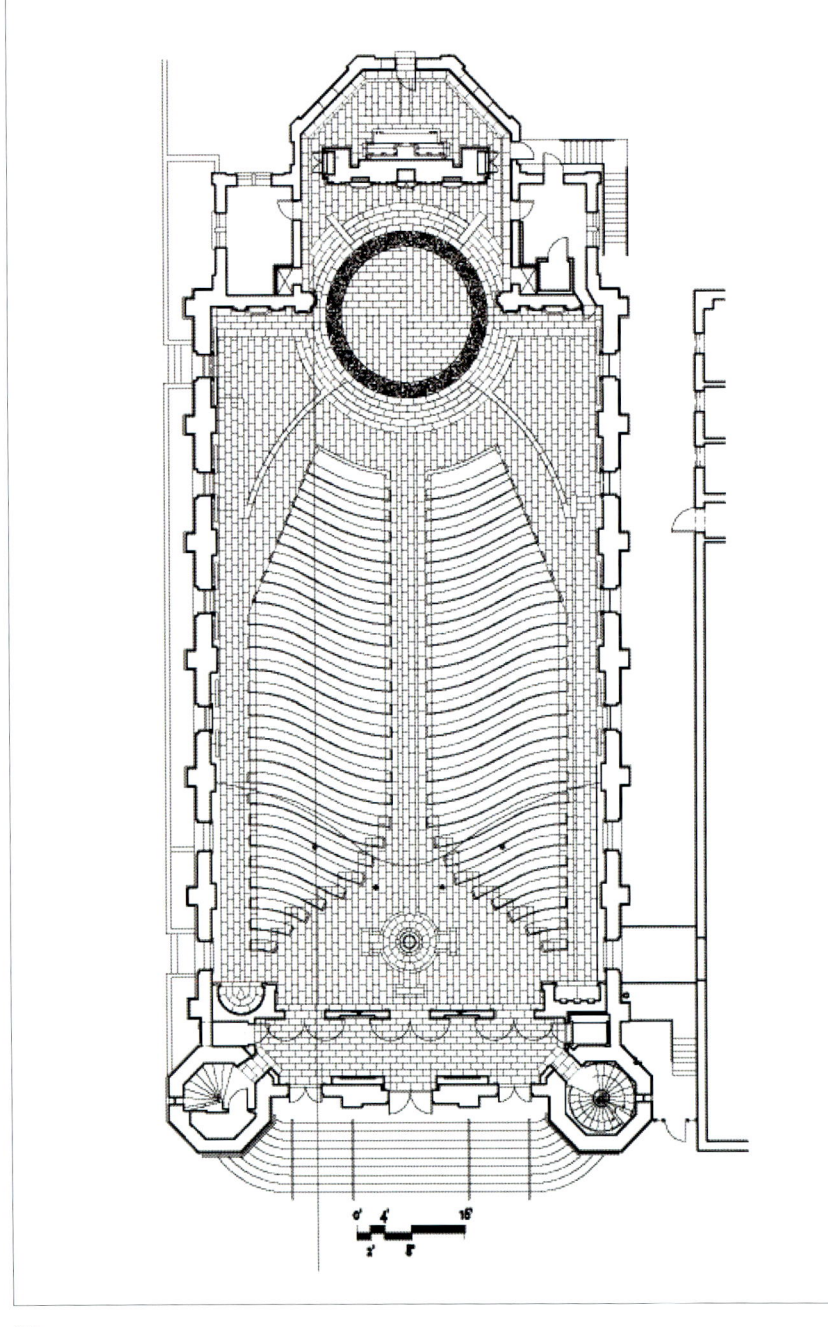

The pastor of Old St. Patrick's Church, Rev. Jack Wall, understood that the restoration of this church's sanctuary required a gentle touch but also an emphatic one. This oldest surviving church in Chicago had remnants of a striking "Irish Renaissance" design, with Celtic-ornamented stained glass made between 1912 and 1922 and modeled after the ancient Book of Kells. But it had been neglected, and much of the larger design was all but erased subsequently in lean decades for the parish.

Old St. Pat's had come up in the world in recent years, along with its neighborhood near the Loop, and Rev. Wall chose a plan devised by Booth Hansen to recreate its spirit from the early 20th century with many newly wrought elements. By the 1990s, only the stained glass windows could guide the new Celtic design. Their ornate floriated designs inspired an overall make-over in what Larry was convinced could recreate designer Thomas O'Shaughnessy's intent almost 90 years before.

Larry's past as a sculptor made him well-suited to designing a richly ornamental space. He enlisted the assistance of an architect-artist, Giselle Taxil, who had attended design school at IIT and later developed techniques for recasting ornament from the work of Louis Sullivan. Together they studied the illumination of the Book of Kells, analyzed remnants of wall stencils, and made watercolors to propose new ornament. Their freehand designs were transferred to CAD, and the computer produced full-size drawings to cut molds for plaster work. These images were also employed as templates for marble work that employed water jet technology to cut stone precisely and economically.

The sense of timeless craftsmanship is present in many elements—such as the stenciling that runs up the walls and across trusses. The designs in the altar screen—the renovation's masterpiece—are as intricate as any inspired by both O'Shaughnessy and Irish tradition. But the imagery also has a simplicity which expresses a "kind of minimalism," said artist Giselle, that touches the high tech spirit as well as the ancient one. "A marriage of meaningful design, new technology and old fashion craftsmanship," was how Larry described it.

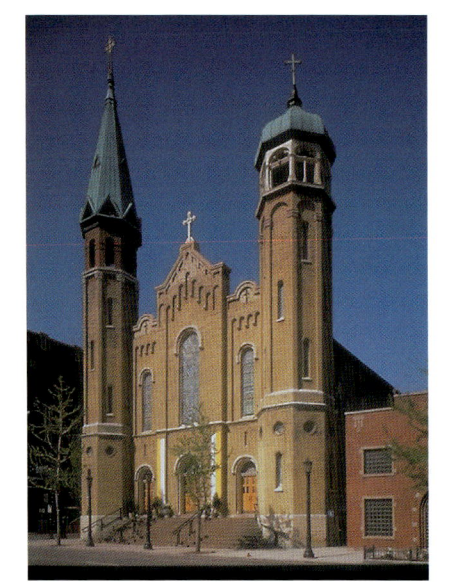

The renovation of the oldest religious building in Chicago expresses humanity on many levels, including the new floor plan.

Right: The Celtic Revival, revived again by Booth Hansen, reaches back to the 11th century.

Below: The objective was to envelop worshippers in color and form by amplifying surviving elements of the classic Celtic interior.

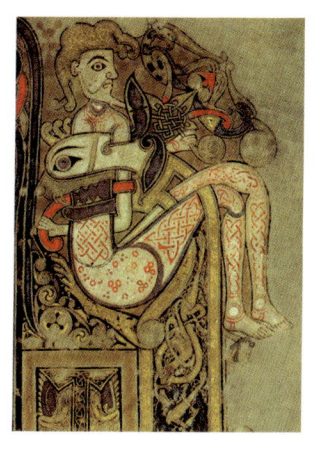

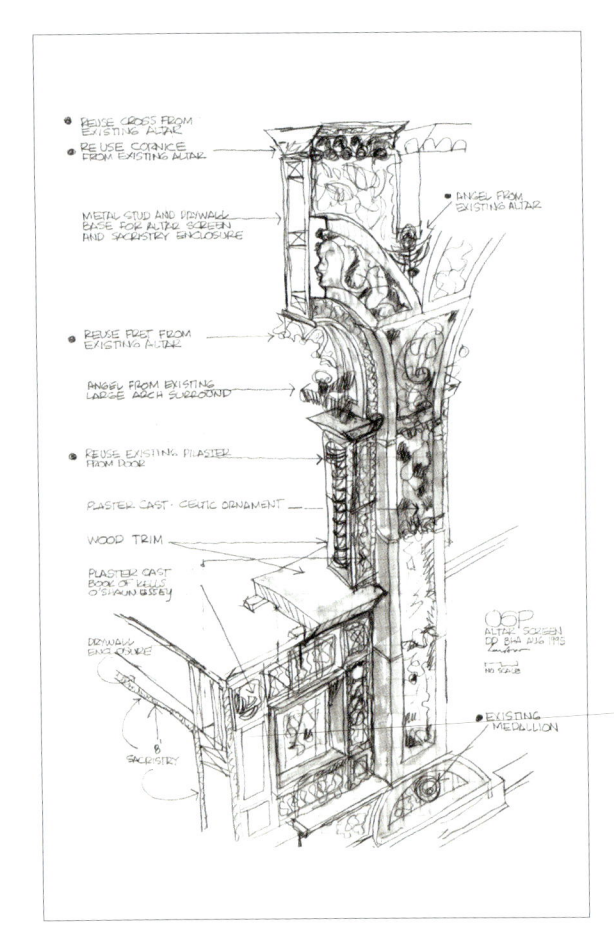

The altar screen is an original design that blends Booth Hansen's technical knowledge and grasp of the spirit of the past.

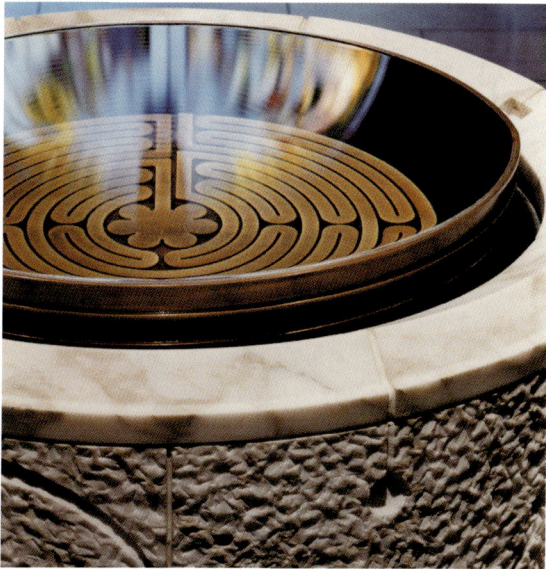

In St. Pat's floor plan and in its details, restraint was necessary as was the courage to fill the senses with color and form.

Cleveland Court

Chicago, 1997

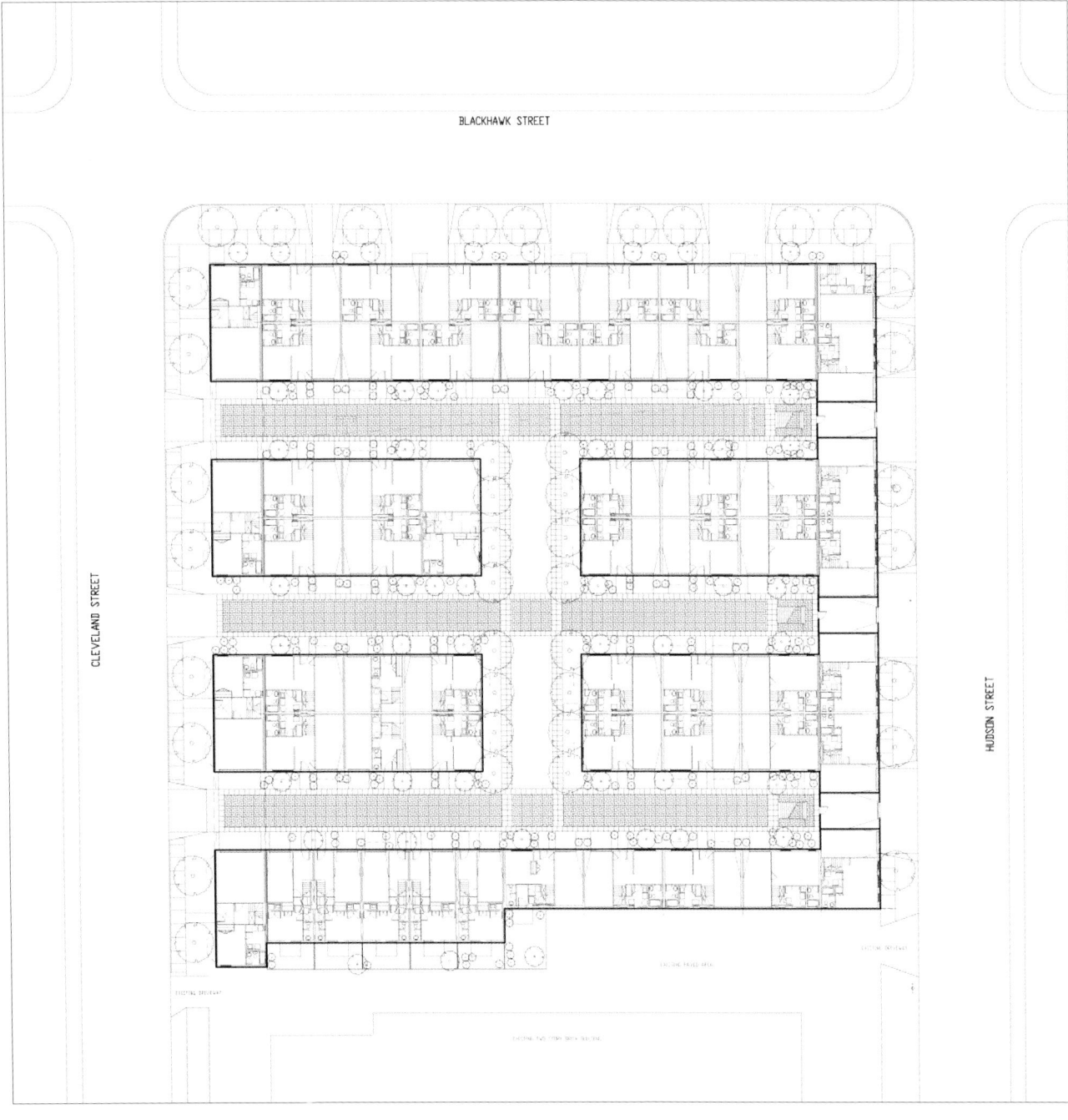

The townhomes of Cleveland Court shifted the typical orientation of attached townhouses (normally perpendicular to the street), here with floor plans 30 feet (or more) wide and 15 feet deep. This achieved many advantages, including the ability to site 57 luxury units on a three-acre site. Interiors are filled with natural light from the front-facing windows, and the plans have amenable circulation with a central staircase. Other distinct selling points include front-access garages and bay windows that in some cases, not all, span two stories.

The economies of the layout were enhanced by fully shared side walls which saved on construction costs and also enabled significant savings on air conditioning and heat. It also made it possible to create a more densely planned complex without sacrificing spaciousness. Ultimately, the selling prices for these units were attractive on the North Side residential market and duly profitable to the developer.

Cleveland Court's plan made optimal use of the space allotted using an unconventional horizontal orientation.

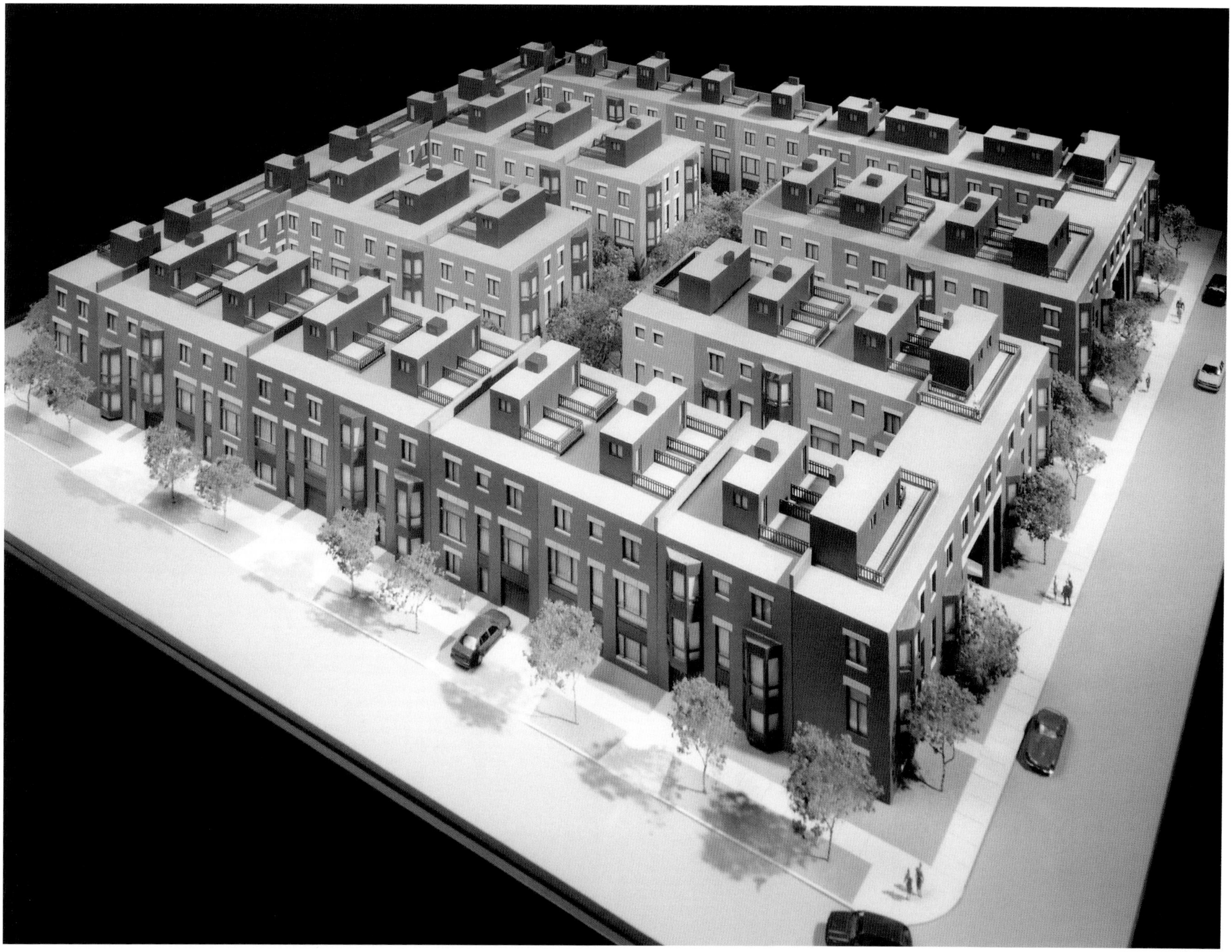

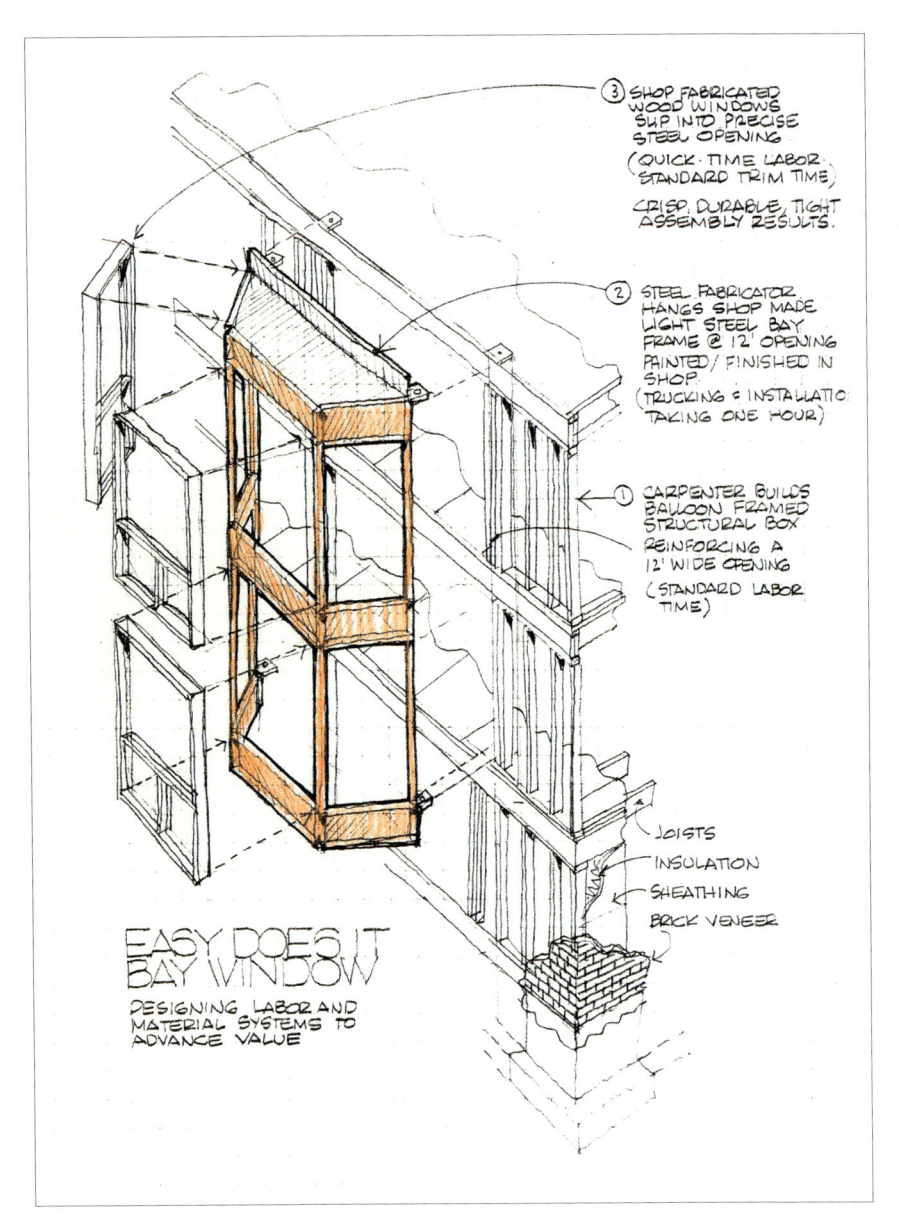

Vertical bay windows enhance spacious interiors. Exterior circulation for pedestrians and automobiles was a key objective.

In a high-density project, simple design is important while details harmonize with historical elements of Lincoln Park.

Cline House

Wheaton, Illinois, 1999

The Cline House benefited from a strong client and evocative site. The client had built a house previously and understood what he could and should ask of an architect. In this case, he was eager to accommodate his extended family, which often visited, with spaces that would be connected but separate. The site was on a golf course, the oldest in the United States, and near an Arts and Crafts clubhouse, aspects of which he wanted to recall. The solution was a series of cottage-like wings connected by a spine, all detailed in a hand-crafted manner.

Division into separate wings was a suitable strategy. They could be scaled to modest profiles, and with varied exposures. They could provide layered views of the golf course and environs. The plan also creates outdoor spaces where the gardens of sedges and wildflowers could infiltrate into the recesses and courtyards. Hand-crafted techniques include a striking series of double-pitched roofs with flared eaves, a throwback to the Tudor Revival in England. Sand-stuccoed walls echo the clubhouse and create a timeless feel despite the large plate-glass windows that enhance views.

Inside, the woodwork is mostly pale maple throughout, simply milled, enhancing the handmade feel. The pitch of the roof overhead has corresponding ceilings which enclose interior space with high ceilings, producing a feeling of spaciousness in the center, and lower, more intimate places around the perimeter.

The double pitch and curving slope of the roofs have a historic feel over an otherwise modern structure.

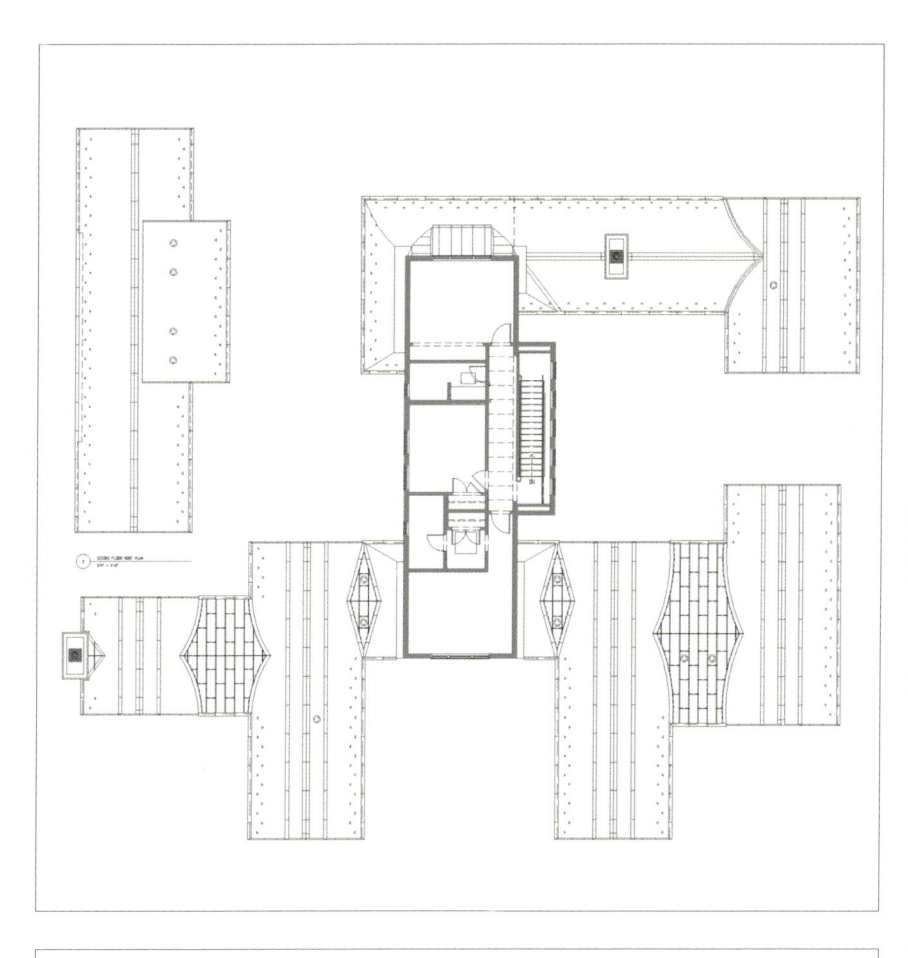

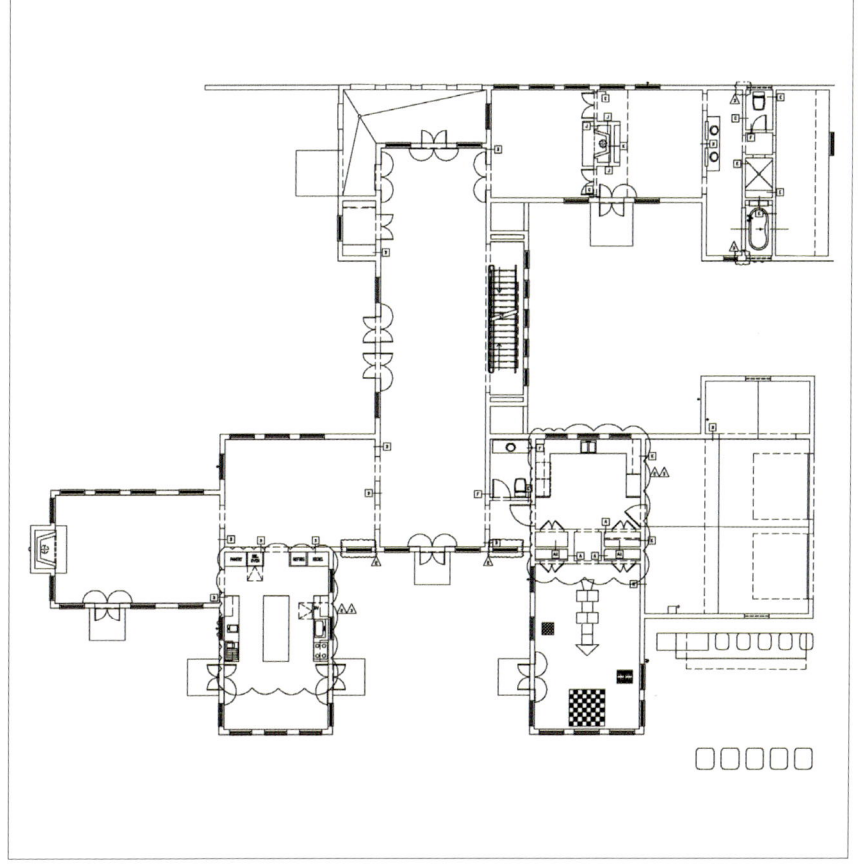

The house is luxurious in size, a sensation amplified by the outdoor spaces of the plan.

It reads as a house which is both historic and modern in spirit.

The varied elevations of the architecture are a suitable setting for multiple terraces and rock gardens.

Each wing has a distinct function for the extended family including grandchildren.

Rusticity is encouraged by the architecture. So are luxuries afforded by open space, such as a more-than-ample kitchen.

Ganz Hall
of the Auditorium Building
Reconstruction, Chicago, 1999

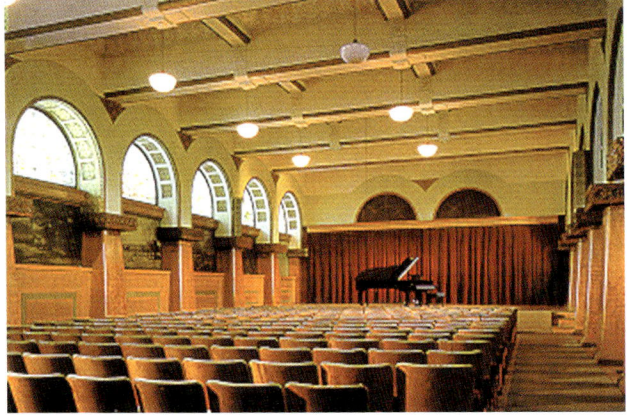

Booth Hansen demonstrated its skill with elaborate detail in this restoration of the gem-like Louis Sullivan-designed space. The recital hall, a part of Sullivan's Auditorium Building, represents the original architect's use of lavish ornamentation in an integrated work. Arcades on both sides open the small space to natural light through stained glass. Short columns have intricate capitals, each unique, alive with carved foliate patterns. Even the beam work is both muscular and delicately detailed.

Despite its many rich details, the space seemed barren without the ten electroliers that appeared in old photos and were suspended from above. Starting with the few period images available, Booth Hansen draftspeople reproduced ten of the cast-metal fixtures. Through digital enhancement, tireless iteration, and close work with a casting studio, the organic quality of the objects was restored to a state of historical accuracy, but more important, a true Sullivanesque feel.

The Auditorium Building's Ganz Hall, originally for recitals, had been altered several times over the years.

The strength of the Richardsonian arch is expressed in the theater entry, restored by Booth Hansen, as it is throughout the building and especially in Ganz Hall.

The ornamentation of the original is unified and restrained despite the rich ornamentation typical of Louis Sullivan's original.

100

Sullivan was modernism's great prophet, hardly for his simplicity, rather for his sense of both proportion and detail, qualities which guided Booth Hansen's recreation of the ten cast metal light fixtures, designed from old photos.

The Chicken Factory
Chicago, 2000

Amplifying an existing spirit is typically an important design objective. Larry often achieves this with traditional details, but in this project he found it in an overall brick structure built for the most practical industrial needs. The loft movement had already showed that genteel dwellings could be carved from industrial buildings. This one was more difficult than most, and required more intensive interventions, but it became striking proof that meaning and spirit reside in found objects.

The brick building had little to suggest renovation except for solid brick walls and a robust smoke stack, part of which now encloses a spiral staircase. The clients believed that the former chicken processing plant could be a comfortable home if the design achieved a few specific things. One was to create a sight line from the front door to the garden in back. This involved cutting new windows and pouring level floors.

The Chicken Factory has an interior plan that both architect and clients unabashedly call "Palladian." This meant that spaces are separate but interlocking, and interior volumes borrow light from the perimeter. In a building that had been asymmetrical, the new main axis and a transverse one enable columns (some load bearing and some not) to establish an organizing grid. "The geometry gives you a sense of balance and order. The axes lead you gently from place to place," Larry told a magazine shortly after the project was completed.

In the order-from-chaos process, it was natural to expose the reinforced concrete beams as design elements, and to affirm the interior rhythm with sections of drywall that float away from the otherwise exposed brick. With the concrete of the floors left raw and adorned with sleek modern furniture, the message of this livable home (which has an added second floor, clad in zinc) is clear. It is that recycling a building of this unlikely kind blends minimalism with romance.

The house began as an industrial building. It is now organized and domesticated around an irregular shape.

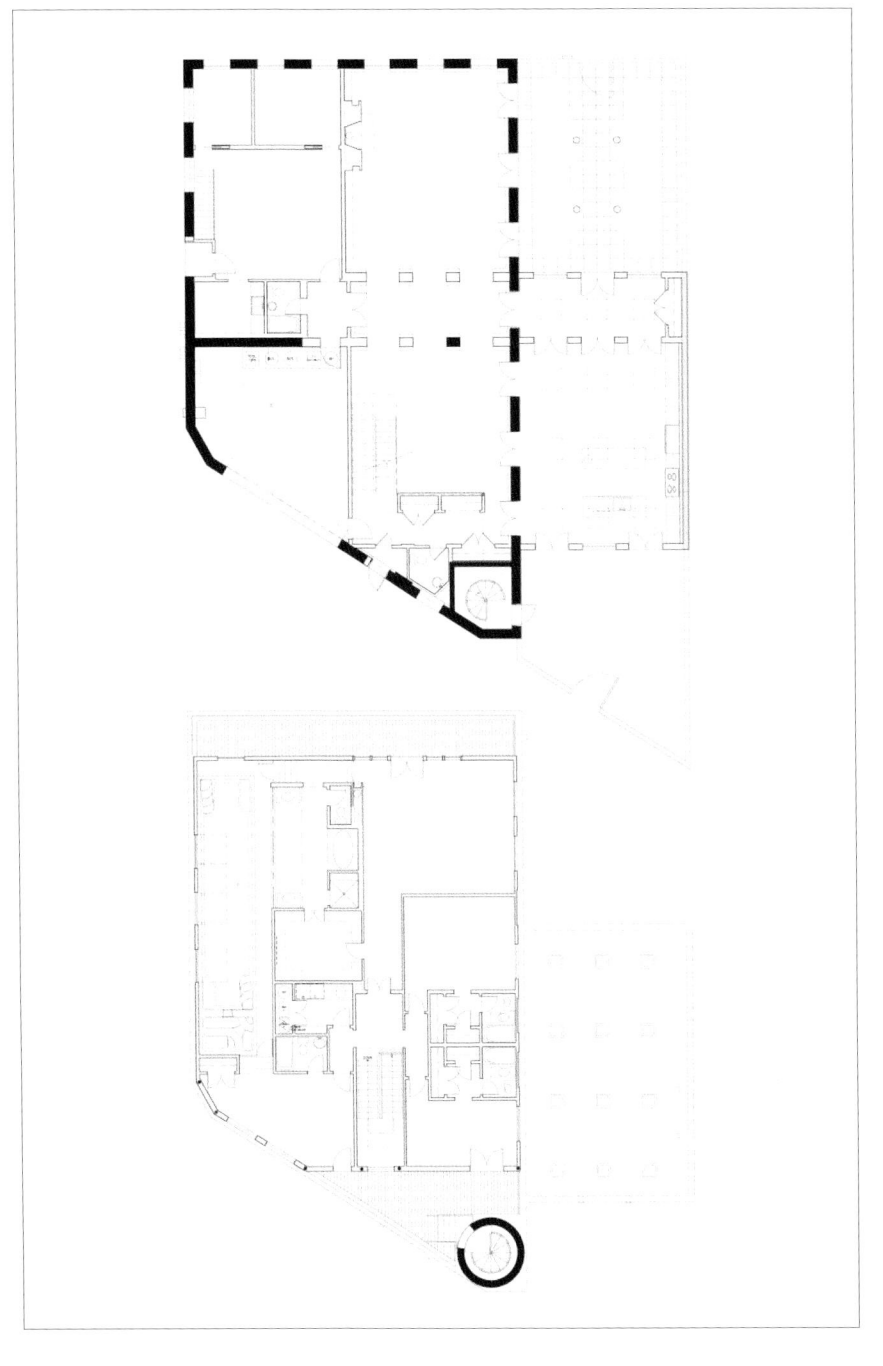

Bringing order to what was a chaotic patchwork of spaces was the objective. The lessons of Palladio applied. So did the stark drama of the Mies-like stairway.

103

Coyne Vocational College
Chicago, 2000

LEGEND:
- CIRCULATION
- ADMINISTRATION/FACULTY
- LOBBY/MULTIPURPOSE
- CLASSROOMS
- BUILDING SERVICES
- STUDENT SUPPORT

FIRST FLOOR PLAN

SECOND FLOOR PLAN

The simple form of the Coyne College building rendered a powerful sense of place for this vocational school just beyond the Loop and on the edge of a railroad right of way. The program and budget required a basic structure with space for classrooms, labs, student amenities and faculty offices. A structure of wide-flange steel beams and pre-cast concrete kept the project economical while creating 80,000 square feet of usable space for the growing school.

The 30-foot-high glass wall of the facade provides natural light for the entry, which filters into classrooms overlooking the triple-high space. Outside, the steel canopy echoes the light tower of the adjacent train tracks while it also creates a metaphorical gateway for a school which enables young students to embark in vocational fields such as air conditioning, electrical maintenance, and other technical trades that are, like this building, both modern and timeless in their usefulness.

The plan's objective was to create a multiplicity of usable spaces in a basic and economical space.

The canopy is gateway-like and provides a sense of ceremony in a utilitarian building.

The grand central atrium brings in light and renders a sense of organization to the interior.

Circulation is clear in an interior that is remarkably animated for a building so underdetailed.

MacLean Museum of Asian Art

Mettawa, Illinois, 2001

For a site on his wooded property near Chicago, industrialist Barry MacLean imagined a museum for his vast collection of Chinese ceramics, made over the years as he traveled to Asia on business. Before meeting Larry, MacLean had commissioned another architect who designed a Chinese inflected building, which Barry did not like well enough to build. Then he discussed the problem with Larry, and they discovered that the client was emotionally tied to the oak savanna of his property, and he wanted that reflected in the museum.

The answer was a structure, or series of structures, modeled loosely on the simple lines of a Midwestern pole barn. This would enable a variety of spaces, from open storage to dramatic displays for large objects.

The museum has the simplicity of an Illinois barn but is rendered distinct and even otherworldly by stele serving as columns.

The barn idea also lent itself to a layout not unlike a Chinese hutong, or multi-family residence laid out with many courtyards to create maximum exposure to the outside and cross ventilation. The floor plan of the museum expresses Asian values such as repose and layered views of the outside world.

Various entries to the building are connected by a breezeway, typically American if not Midwestern, and characteristic in residential architecture. Plain posts or columns might typically line such an indoor-outdoor feature. For this one, MacLean had stone stele carved, each one different, to use as supports for the overhang. As the design developed and was built, client and architect were pleased that the subtle charms of rural Illinois could be touched with sublime harmonies of Chinese art and a universal tone.

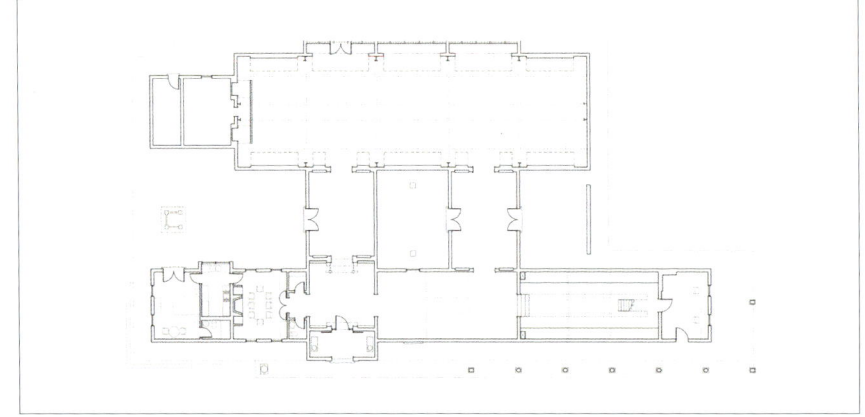

It is imposing, as barns sometimes are on the Midwestern landscape. It is subtlely divided like a Chinese hutong into spaces of various sizes and with courtyards that increase air and light inside.

The larger spaces of the MacLean Museum serve variously as open storage and as dramatic exhibit galleries.

111

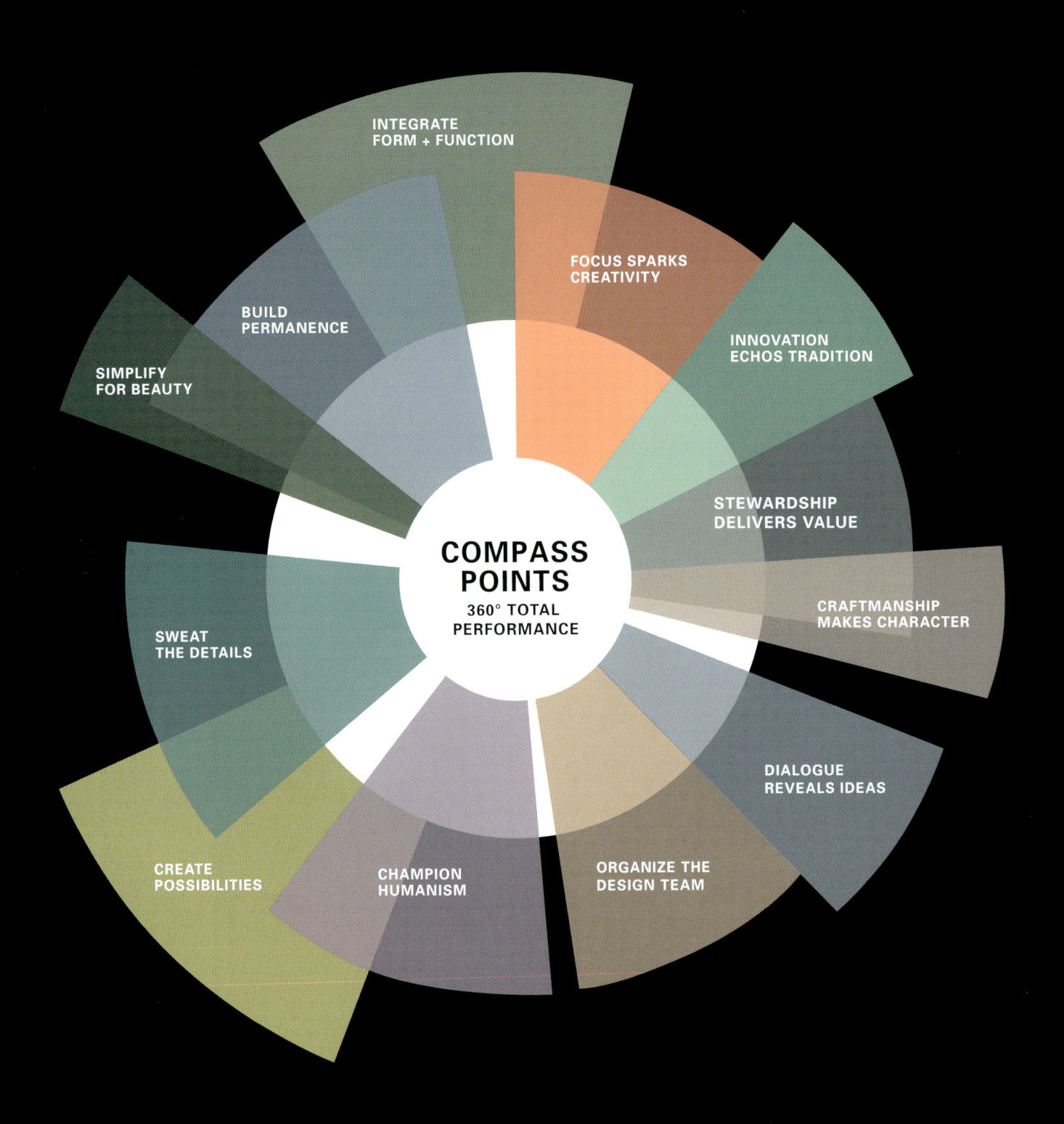

COMPASS POINTS
360° TOTAL PERFORMANCE

- INTEGRATE FORM + FUNCTION
- FOCUS SPARKS CREATIVITY
- INNOVATION ECHOS TRADITION
- STEWARDSHIP DELIVERS VALUE
- CRAFTMANSHIP MAKES CHARACTER
- DIALOGUE REVEALS IDEAS
- ORGANIZE THE DESIGN TEAM
- CHAMPION HUMANISM
- CREATE POSSIBILITIES
- SWEAT THE DETAILS
- SIMPLIFY FOR BEAUTY
- BUILD PERMANENCE

All fundamental values of architecture lead to the same goal: total performance.

Total Performance
Excelling by Every Measure

Insight often deepens when one least expects it, as happened one evening in the 1990s when Larry Booth attended a reception at the Art Institute of Chicago. Larry was introduced to a new acquaintance, and after the normal pleasantries, the gentleman asked, "What kind of architecture do you practice?" It was hardly a complicated question, but Larry did not have a ready answer.

His firm Booth Hansen had never been easy to categorize, and less so as its commissions expanded to include a wider range of building types, from houses in the suburbs to commercial buildings in the city. The firm had won recognition in many kinds of architecture, and the flow of work that followed was changing the scale of the firm, if not its disciplined approach.

Larry smiled, thought for a moment, then broke the silence. "We do high performance architecture," he said. He imagined that this would call up ready images of sleek, shiny automobiles, which was not a perfect analogy. Larry was patient enough to mention a couple of projects that they had recently done, and the new acquaintance walked off, apparently satisfied.

For Larry, what tripped off of his tongue as a quip, "high performance," had more meaning than he first suspected. Performance was in fact an essential benchmark for his firm, and it described succinctly the objective of any commission they undertook. This was not new. For nearly 30 years at that time, the firms that Larry headed had achieved excellence through a process of establishing goals and meeting them. The objective was a refined architecture which satisfied a wide range of criteria.

At the office, Larry started referring to the goal as "total performance," and it became more resonant as Booth Hansen was paying attention to standards of excellence that were more exacting, especially in larger work where functionality is often closely measured. Architects were increasingly responsible for innovation as building technology advanced more swiftly than ever before. They were also considered stewards of the environment, as buildings were increasing judged by their "carbon footprint." Clients and the public at large, moreover, were more demanding aesthetically.

"How can we guarantee total performance every time?" Scott Cyphers, a Booth Hansen partner, asked in a meeting to discuss a new, complex commission that had just come to the office.

"We sweat the details," said an associate, repeating an expression that Larry liked to use.

Early sketches and notes made by Larry while preparing proposals for an art center in Champaign, Illinois and for a mechanized postal facility at O'Hare Airport.

"We have checklists," Scott said.

"Does that mean every detail hits the mark?" Larry asked. He knew the answer.

"Not every one," said Scott.

"Everyone needs to be on the same page," Larry said. "Maybe we need better flow charts."

As the total performance concept developed, new and more detailed flow charts were devised, these being "road maps" to get the project from design concept to final construction. The idea was that an exacting step-by-step process would make sure, for example, that HVAC equipment was integrated with the structural system. More to the point, the Quality Track System, as Booth Hansen called the enhanced work flow, told everyone on the team, including the contractors and tradespeople, exactly when their work was critical.

"Does that assure high performance?" Scott asked.

"No, but it gives everyone a better chance to solve problems," Larry said.

"Creatively solve problems," said the associate.

Creativity had always been a keynote at Booth Hansen, and now people were asking the practical question of how creativity could be managed. The answer, Larry believed, would be in a clear statement of precepts—basic architectural principles—in plain language and not jargon, so fundamental that they could apply to any element of design.

Making such a list was not instantaneous. It required time, and trial and error. Ultimately Larry and colleagues listed twelve "compass points," as he called them, simply stated. They would inspire action, elicit collaboration and help set standards. Each compass point could guide the large outlines of a project. It could also help refine detail. Often it would do both.

It was no mere coincidence that the establishment of Compass Points was codified as the Booth Hansen office acquired large urban

Booth Hansen studio, Desplaines Street, Chicago

In a conference room with drawings all around, where much creative work is accomplished.

commissions which were technically complex. As more people and more professions were involved, they called for what is often regarded as the first compass point: *organize teamwork*. This stresses the importance of broad participation, including clients, engineers and others who bring critical input to projects. Teamwork was indispensable in the 2018 apartment building, The Parker in Chicago's West Loop. In early discussions, the team discussed objectives and their roles in meeting them. They agreed, among other things, that the 30-story Parker must provide the best possible views all around, and all successive decisions would support that goal.

Another compass point, *simplify for beauty*, helped bring forth The Parker's neat parabolic profile. *Integrate form and function* affirmed the idea that balconies could be integrated into the structure, not hung against it. These sometimes obvious injunctions led to simple gestures that might have gotten lost without agreed upon principles that enforced purity of form.

Another Booth Hansen project in Chicago applied other compass points with notable success. The luxury condominiums at 61 East Banks Street had a key design breakthrough when the team endeavored to *create possibilities*, meaning to propose multiple solutions for any problem. In this case, it led to an uncommon plan with two-story townhouses around the base of the eight-story building. *Innovation echoes tradition* inspired projecting bay windows, a modern element that admits light and opens space, and which harks back to the old Chicago School.

It is not that the compass points are themselves magical, rather they represent timeless elements of the design process which have inspired beautiful buildings of many kinds through many eras. They encourage architects to understand even complex architecture as a breakdown of simple elements assembled in the most suitable way possible.

Nor is it that the twelve compass points are exhaustive. Rather, they provide a framework for refinement, and a reminder that creative solutions do not normally come like a bolt of lightning.

Compass Points encourages a step-by-step process, orderly but never twice the same. The ideal result is a work of art as beautiful as if it could have been designed in no other way than that which was created by a team which remains focused together and in concert.

Republic Windows and Doors

Chicago, 1998

The owners of Republic Windows and Doors were crystal clear with Booth Hansen about what they wanted in a new factory. It would substantially improve the conditions of the workplace, also enhance the historic Goose Island industrial district. What resulted is an innovative factory design, noted for its space and light, also a sense of order and dignity wrought of basic and unadorned materials. Booth Hansen project architect David Mann and Larry agreed that a humane factory could be achieved less with an increase in expense and more through a direct understanding of the needs of the company and its people.

In many ways, the humane factory is also a minimal one. It is a 350,000-square-foot box with forty-foot bays that enable work to be spread out. It is also flexible as the nature and organization of the work is certain to change over time. Seemingly simple features made big differences in getting what clients and workers wanted. The front facade is largely transparent, as Republic's management sought to be itself. The sides and back have exposed supports, and corrugated steel cladding is suspended behind them, highlighting structure and creating an artistic and lively exterior profile. Inside, the main workspace has a spacious central atrium with a perimeter of seven-foot-high clerestories overhead which bring abundant natural light throughout the factory floor.

Other humane solutions were equally straightforward and economic. The entry space and adjacent offices are behind a portico of basic steel columns and glass wall. It is unornamented but a dignified and civilizing influence, as Larry stressed. Parking for all is in front, and the loading docks flank the entry, which (in addition to keeping shipping orderly) highlights the fact that the work of the factory and other aspects of the business, including management, are intermingled. An emphatic icon is a monumental bare-steel staircase in the triple-high entry hall which is used by both office and factory workers. It is symbolic and both industrial and democratic in character.

When the owners of Republic embarked on their new building, openness would be a keynote of the building they imagined

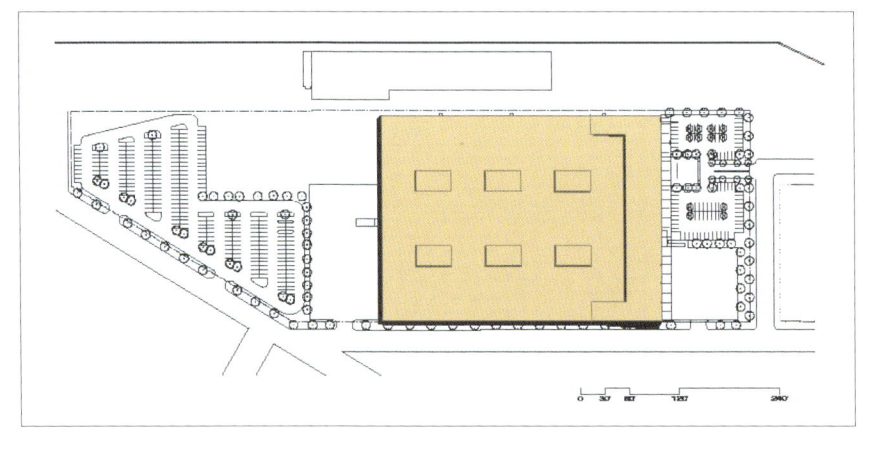

Parking is not hidden, and the loading docks are part of the facade that Republic presents to the world.

117

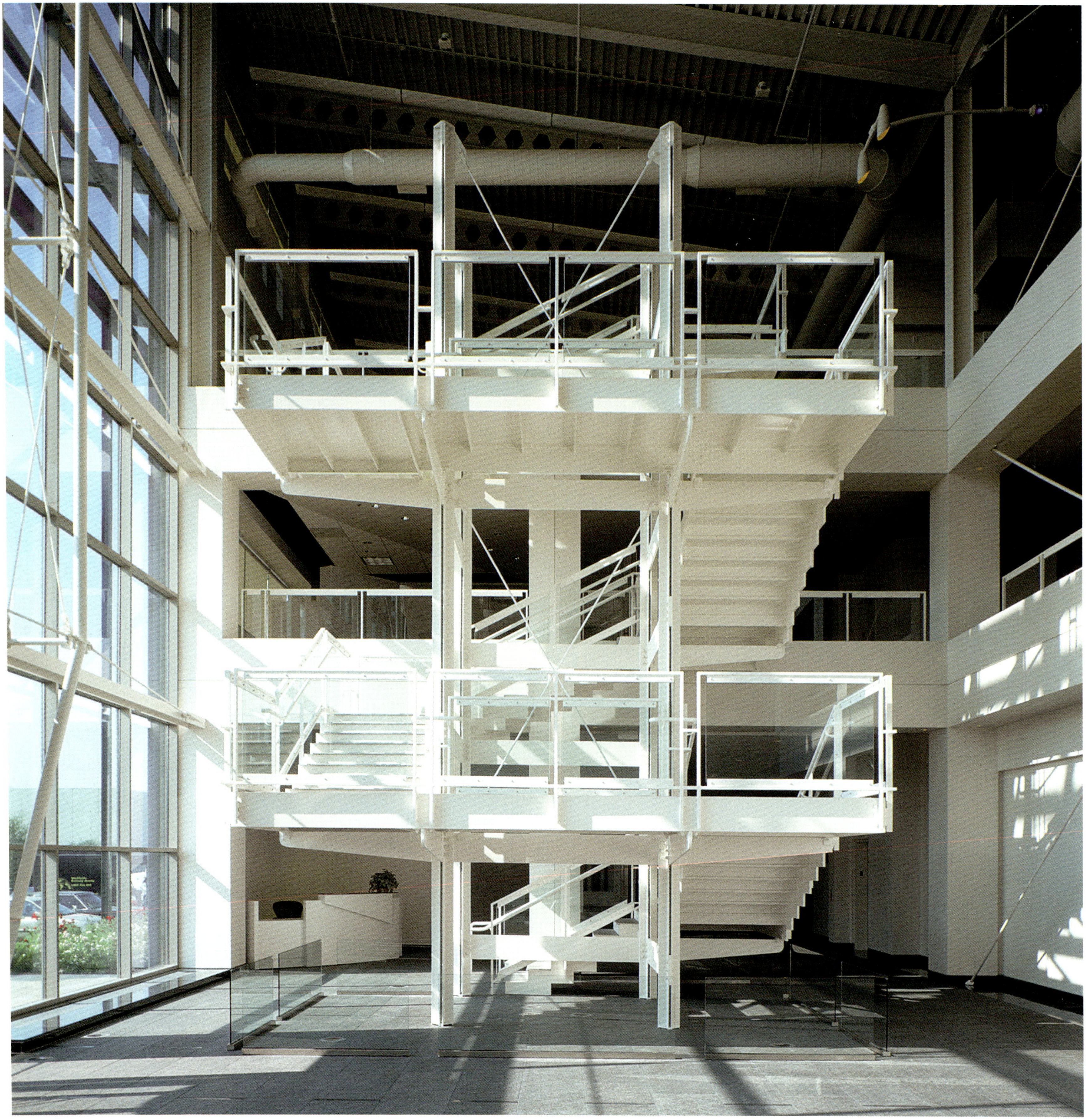

The iconic industrial stairway in the atrium lobby is for workers and managers alike.

Above: Clerestories bring more-than-ample light to the factory floor.

Left: Glass wall admits abundant natural light into the entry

School of the Art Institute of Chicago

Student Residences, Chicago, 2000

When the high-rise dormitory of the School of the Art Institute appeared in the year 2000, it was a surprise in the Loop where most new skyscrapers were going up with orthogonal profiles and glassy curtain walls. The Art Institute building reached back to the old Chicago School. A more understated surprise was that the design and construction of the building was innovative in many ways.

As Booth Hansen researched the elements of an ideal modern residence, they discerned that 13-foot units were adaptable to a variety of dormitory configurations. They further discovered that the 13-foot organizing bay, a convention used by Chicago School architects, was flexible and adaptable to a variety of uses for the "commercial style" of the late 19th century. The intriguing confluence led to a design of modern functionality and a profile, and a 17-story height, that recalls the Loop when it was home to architecture's earliest skyscrapers.

Other innovative means were used in construction, including reverting to a steel frame, as used in the past, because the tightness of the site made a poured concrete set up impractical. Over this "bridge frame," the architects used panels of an innovative cast material that was economical, light and easily assembled. The result was a building that resembles the Chicago School in many ways, but is as well-suited to its purpose as its sleek and modern neighbors.

The School of the Art Institute building is sited in Chicago's historic Loop.

The school's residential and classroom functions are housed in a modern building that adapted historic construction technologies and drew its profile from the Loop skyscrapers of the past.

Kohl Museum

Glenview, Illinois, 2005

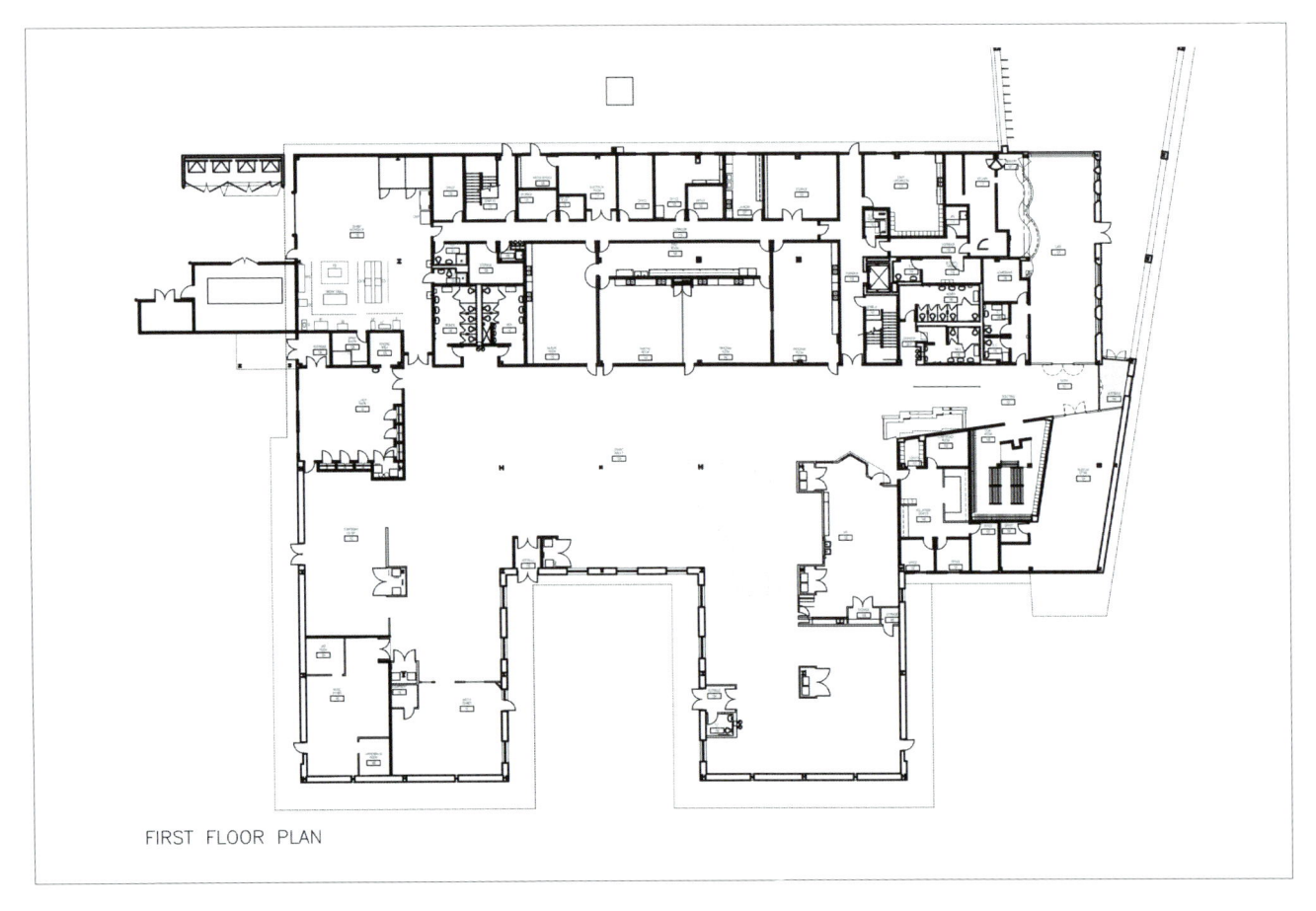

Buildings often communicate messages as well as provide shelter, and the Kohl Museum, a place where children learn as they play, made an ecological message a key element of the architecture. The site is notable: an expansive prairie with native grasses amidst an otherwise built-up suburb. The building sits comfortably, not invasively, on the site. The wing-like roofline which evokes birds in flight highlights the spaciousness of the site and the freedom of the learning experience within.

Among subjects addressed by the museum is sustainability, lessons of which are reinforced by a series of recycled materials, also with wide clerestory windows which provide ample natural light and minimize artificial illumination. The building has solar panels conspicuous and well integrated into the south-facing roof. While the LEED Silver certificate of the building is unlikely to impress the youngest visitors, the conscientious environmental design of the building has many aesthetic and functional notes which evoke curiosity and transmit the idea that good buildings should be harmonious with the greater environment.

FIRST FLOOR PLAN

Kohl's floor plan incorporates offices, exhibition space and access to the outdoors. The wing-like profile dominates a broad prairie and pierces the sky.

The entry is an emphatic sign that this is a place of wonder.

The architecture draws visitors forth.

The building has clarity, simplicity and sustainability.

Below and opposite:
The interiors of the museum feature diversity and elicit curiosity.

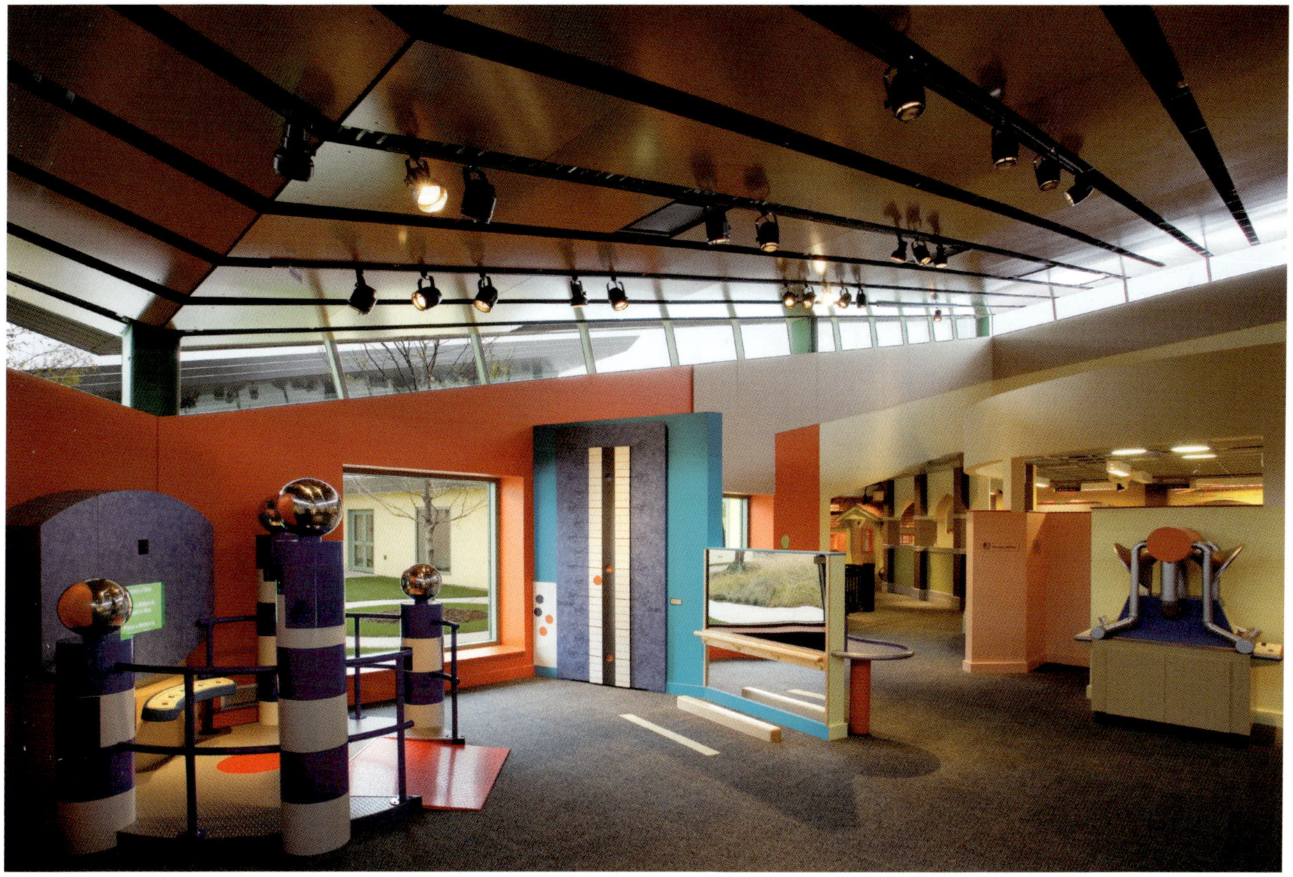

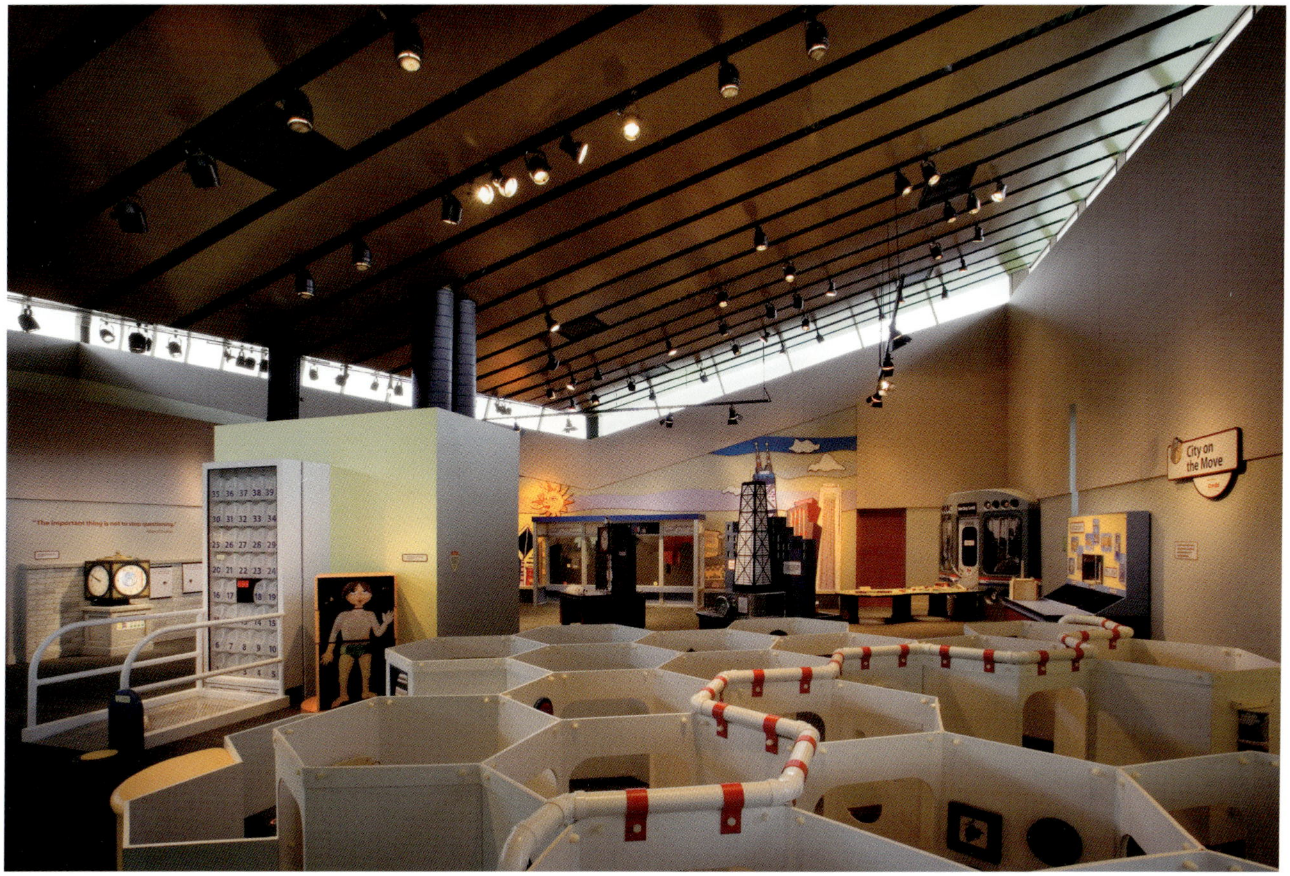
City on the Move

Joffrey Tower
Chicago, 2005

Named for the international dance company that has studios in the building, Joffrey Tower was designed with rationalist rigor wherein interior spaces drive the exterior expression. It also represents a suitable response to the urbanistic density of its central Loop site. Program requirements were complex and challenging. Commercial space would go into the first eight floors with longspan spaces, and residences above them to the top at the 32nd floor. The building also needed to harmonize with a streetscape which has the mid-rise Marshall Field's building, across Randolph Street, as its centerpiece.

Booth Hansen's solution was a straightforward and simple profile which belies the complexity of the project. The steel framing enables a grid which reveals structure, expresses the varied functions within, and provides a vivid and animated surface. A terrace between the "pedestal" and the "tower" provides an intermediate roofline that corresponds with Field's across the street. Condominiums with narrower floor plates and tighter grid are raised on pilotis, raising the living spaces over the commercial base and above the view-blocking parking garage between the Joffrey and Lake Michigan. This gesture refers, if only obliquely, to the graceful legs of the dancers associated with the building's signature tenant.

At State and Randolph Streets, the project was designed with Joffrey Ballet as its signature tenant. The studios are located in the commercial base of the building with the residential tower above climbing to the 32nd floor.

Left: Like some Chicago buildings, Joffrey Tower amplifies outdoor space with a terrace and greenery.

Above: Modern in glass and steel, Joffrey harmonizes with the Loop's long history.

SoNo Tower

Chicago, 2005

In an area of the North Side that boasts an industrial past, and still features vestiges of it, SoNo ("South of North Avenue") upholds the spirit of the Goose Island district with a minimalism that is both conspicuously functional and elegantly wrought. The structural engineering employed post-tensioned concrete to create thin floor slabs. Wide-flange steel used in the formwork is exposed on spandrels, supports economic window walls, and highlights the unembellished nature of the of the building.

Combined with the structural system is a sense of space within, starting with the integrated balconies, set-back columns, and transparent vision glass. The openness highlights the light-filled and unencumbered spaces typical of modern urban residences–this includes the lobbies and outdoor garden spaces around the entries. These too, feature the unornamented spirit of historic Goose Island, of which SoNo is now a prominent part.

SoNo has the look of a sleek machine in a district that was once fully industrial.

Left: Its glassy exterior suggests a well-lighted space within.

Below: Its technologies assure openness and a variety of interesting spaces for living.

Cook County Circuit Court

Family Division, Chicago, 2005

This was designed to be a gentle building both inside and out, in its visible elements and its invisible ones. The original structure was built more than 100 years before as an industrial loft. The repurposed building now serves cases connected to family disputes and domestic violence. The new building was designed to be calming, peaceful and dignified with a new facade of both openness and formality. Between the new facade and the former outside wall, an atrium extends to the full height of the building. Natural light fills the space which provides separate entries for disputants in delicate cases.

This was the first county building to be designed and constructed after the passage of Chicago's Green Building Ordinance. Natural light filters abundantly into the interior, aided by the soft-colored wooded paneling in the atrium, and by strategically placed clerestories above.

The new facade is constructed of a state-of-the-art rain screen which captures rain water for the building's reuse. Mechanical systems are in line with the building's LEED Silver certification, and photovoltaic panels on the roof provide for a portion of the building's energy needs. The most important sustainability element of the court house was the repurposing of an old building and its embedded energy, which is too often neglected in public architecture.

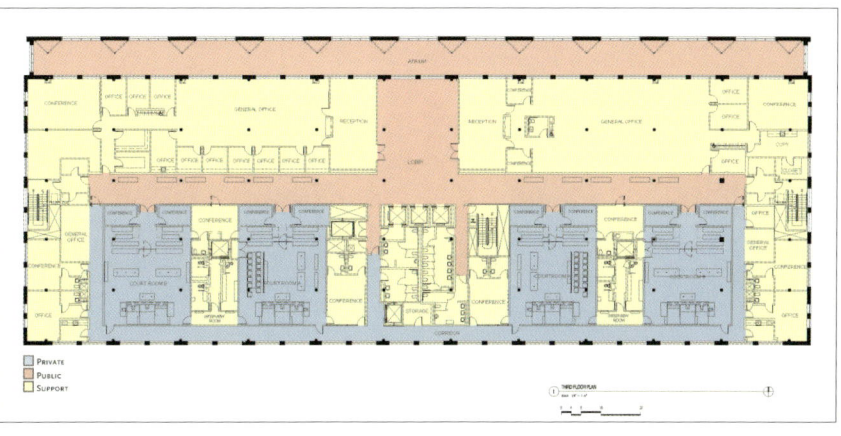

Once an industrial building on the edge of downtown Chicago, its proportions are familiar and its fenestration reassuring.

The courthouse was designed for accessibility, even friendliness, appreciated by people entering family court.

Its long and high atrium entry is bathed in light. It enables litigants involved in cases to use separate entries.

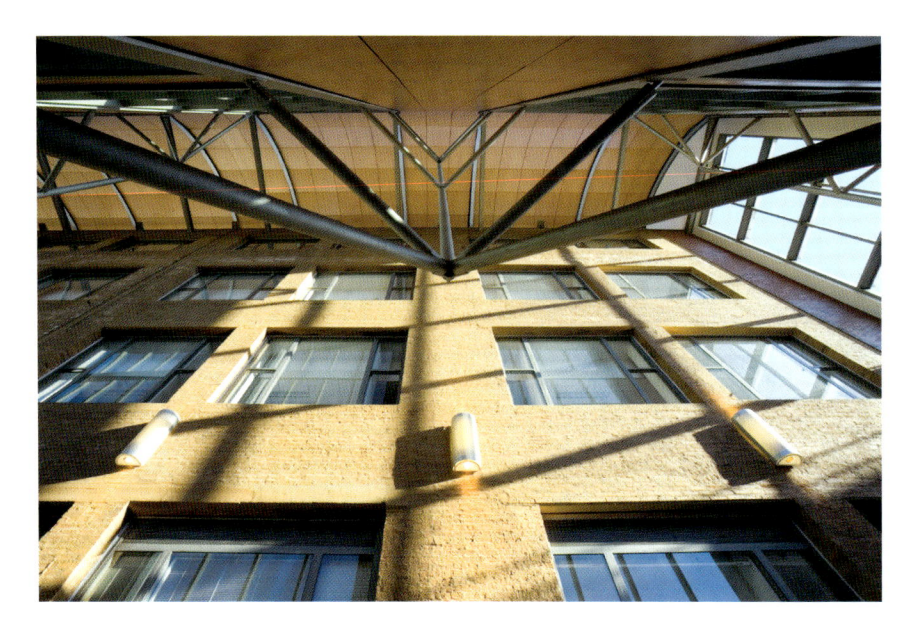

134

Spaces in the family court are designed for openness and calm.

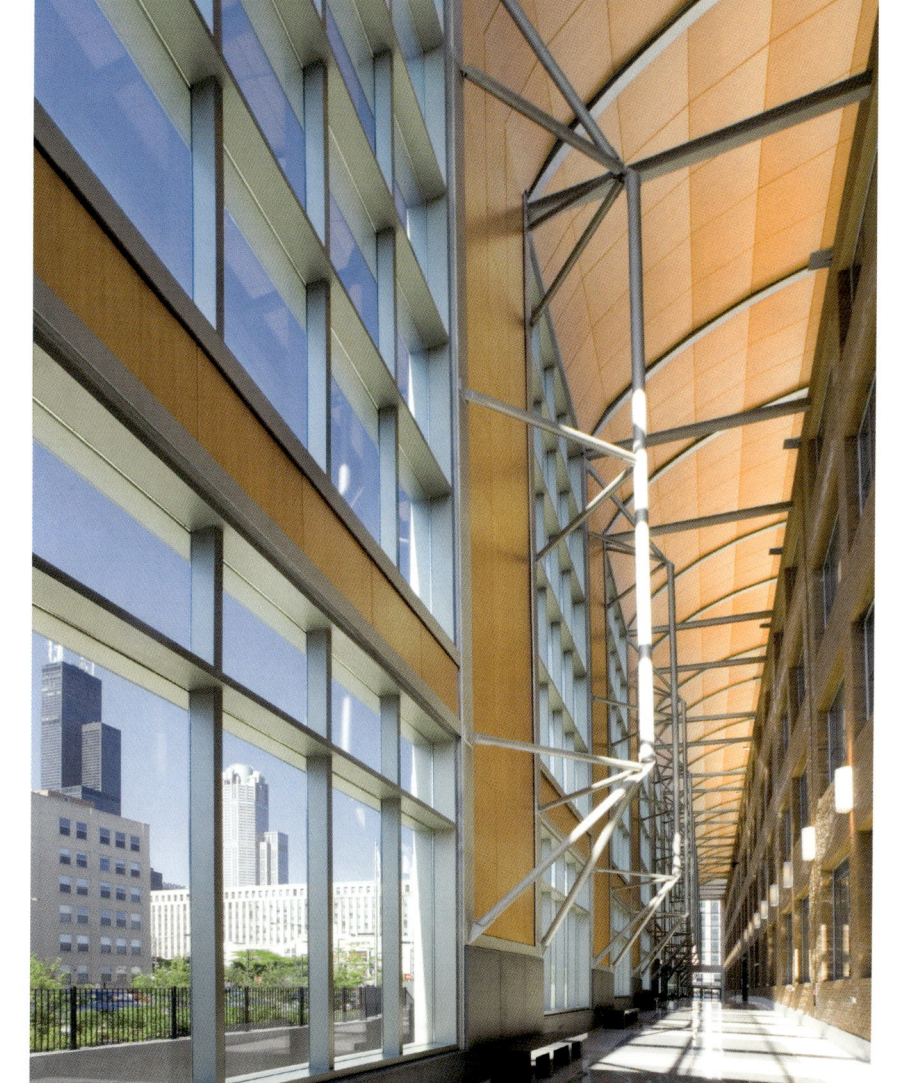

135

Bucksbaum House

Chicago, 2006

The Bucksbaum House occupies a site on a street with mostly historic structures. Context called for ashlar. It is a large house of simplicity and a modernity veiled in gardens and foliage.

The clients sought a spacious house at a scale suitable to the once-modest neighborhood. Thus, the facade is divided into two sections with a courtyard in between. This creates the largest of several garden spaces around the perimeter, a mild buffer between house and street. Large windows and steel-frame bay windows contribute to a thoroughly modern design which maintains scale and palette, including limestone ashlar, in keeping with the neighborhood.

While maintaining a certain intimacy with the neighborhood, the interior plan features double-high space, an open staircase, and axial sightlines that open the interior to the landscaping outside. The result is an interior spaciousness, if not grandeur, which is belied by the low-key exterior profile behind carefully planted gardens visible from the street.

Projections and recesses in the plan expand the feel of the house through glass walls and into garden courtyards.

The structure and spirit of the house enable freedom from end to end and floor to floor.

30 West Oak Street

Chicago, 2006

The objective of the 30 West Oak design was ample space inside and minimal visual disruption in the neighborhood.

The slightly curved profile of 30 West Oak Street, an uncommon form in high-rise architecture in Chicago, achieves several objectives that were discussed by client and architect as they started the design for this 48-unit tower. One was that the curve moderates the effect of its massing on neighbors, both visually and in terms of shadowing. It also enhances views in apartments by providing varied sightlines from different points in the parabola.

Aside from its noteworthy shape, the design was innovative in its approach to the poured-in-place concrete structure. In this case the form work at the curved edge of each slab included a steel beam which was left exposed and provided a precise sill for window walls of each floor. This represented an economical construction technique. It also brings a measure of grid-like organization to the facade, making the tower characteristically "Chicago" in profile, with spandrels that are legible at each of 22 stories.

The tower is bisected on its horizontal axis between the glass spaces of its facade and masonry-clad section that includes the service core.

The cantilevered base opens the streetscape, as modern architecture often does.

140

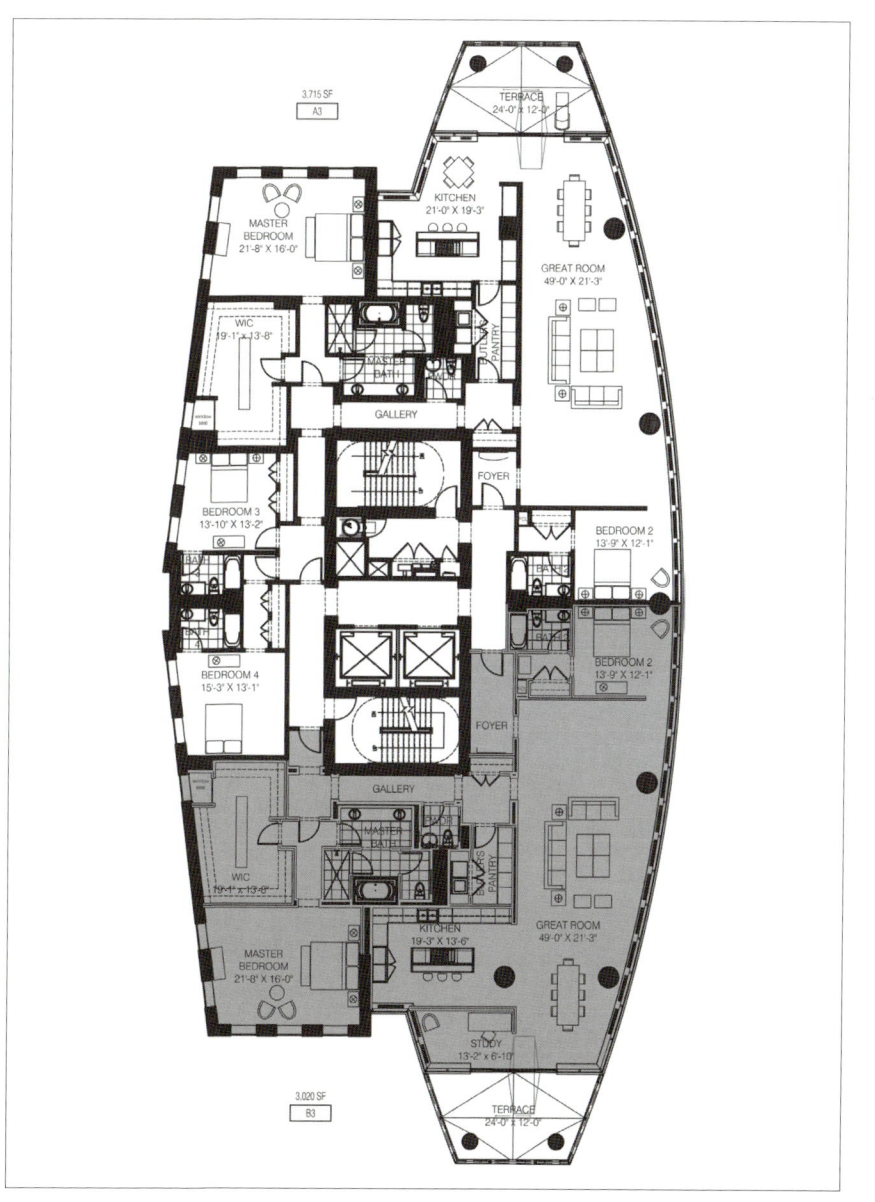

Advanced concrete technology enables maximum space along with economical construction.

Vertical townhouses open on the street beneath the tower of 30 West Oak.

The townhouses share the spirit of the tower: constructivist modernity and the comfort of unbridled space.

Palmolive Residences

Restoration, Chicago, 2008

As in almost any large urban project, the design of new high-end condominiums in one of Chicago's iconic pre-war skyscrapers addressed practical necessity. On 35 stories (above two stories dedicated to retail and commercial use) the developer-client called for approximately 100 living units in spaces that had been offices of largely uniform size. This meant creating layouts of flowing spaces, abundant natural light, acoustical privacy and great views in multiple directions. In order to accommodate modern building systems, floors were raised to create interstitial spaces for new wiring and ductwork, and to effectively lower window sills to provide a more residential feel.

As the Palmolive Building is considered one of the city's great Art Deco landmarks, interiors were designed with sleek detailing to correspond with the streamlined overall design and to express a timeless modernity. Ornament is spare. Oak flooring, polished stone surfaces, artistic tile work and expansive wood paneling employ the mid-20th century concept that has endured into the 21st century. That is to find ornamental beauty in fine materials and straightforward craftsmanship.

The classic is updated with new geometry and dashes of color.

On the original street front, as with Booth Hansen's version, modernizing was designed to suit emphatic merchandising.

Modern lobbies of the Palmolive Building are marked, as in the past, by rich materials.

In the apartments, Booth Hansen designers amplified the space and light that the Palmolive Building featured when it was an office tower.

147

The Parker Fulton Market
Chicago, 2016

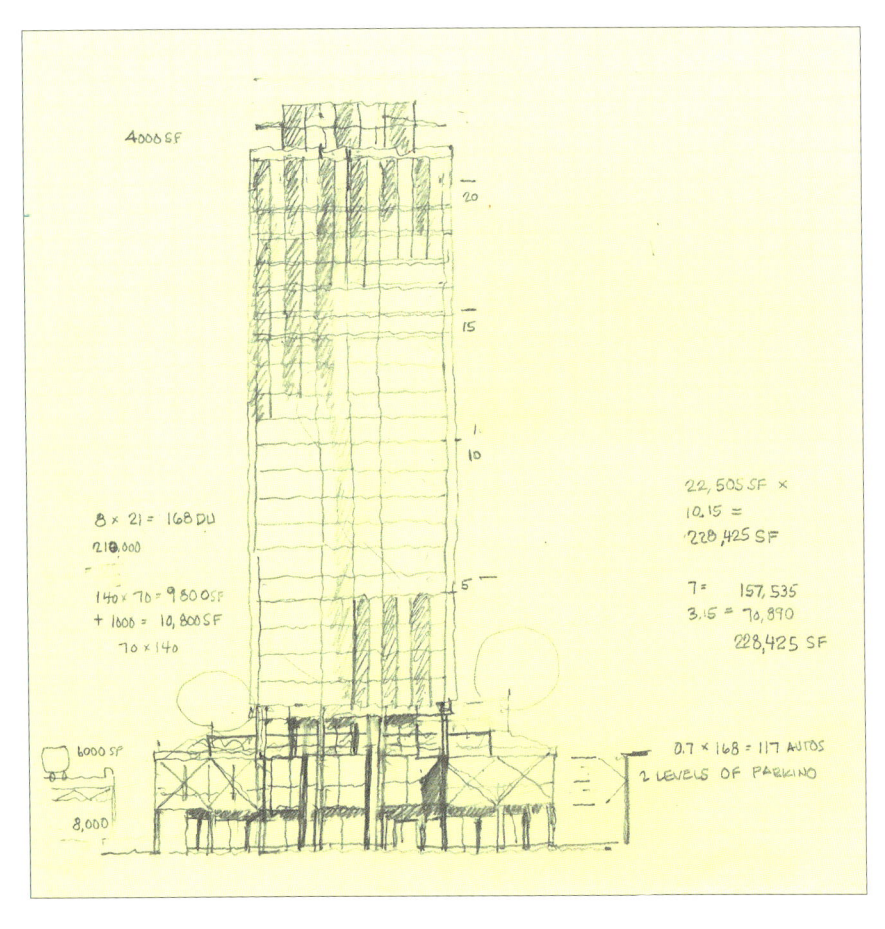

On the edge of the Fulton Market neighborhood, an area of brick lofts, rooftop gardens and fire escapes, The Parker is a sleek residential tower which provides a modern living experience while also integrating itself into the rough-hewn elements of the ex-meatpacking district.

The three-story podium fills the site with service and common areas, and a perimeter mostly lined by pedestrian-friendly retail spaces. The elliptical form of the 29-story tower interlocks with the podium in an irregular way which provides a variety of broad interior spaces on the lower three floors, and terraces with a pool on the podium's landscaped roof.

The tower is massed and positioned to maximize views of the city and the lake's long shore in the distance. Its sleek profile–counterpoint to the rest of the neighborhood shaped over 100 years ago and for industrial use–is enhanced by inset balconies and sheer exterior. Opaque glass slab spandrels highlight the striking geometry, also to suggest construction that reflects the commercial style of the older lofts in the neighborhood. These aesthetic considerations drove the design process along with the programmatic, which involved a variety of apartment layouts, amenities such as fitness center, dog run, lounges and social facilities in the tower penthouse. The distillation and refinement of all elements depended upon the constant collaboration of the design team drawn from a variety of technical professions. All understood the objectives and participated to achieve complex objectives with a simple, striking form.

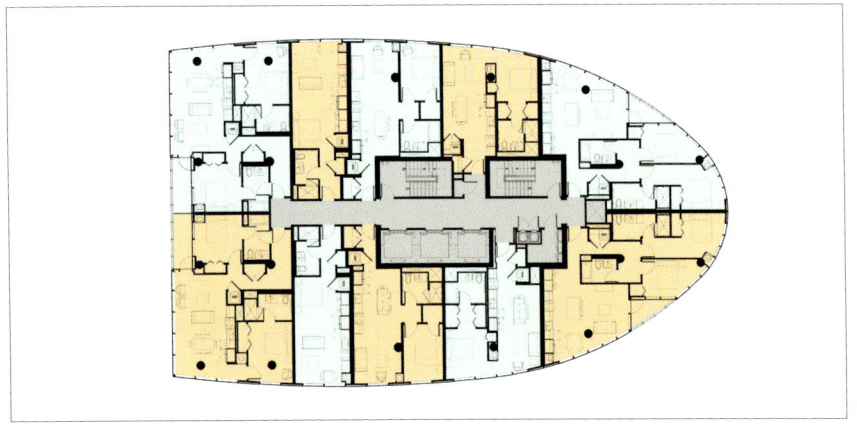

The Parker represented a complex project which was pared down to its simplest possible profile.

At street level, the building is part of an old industrial-commercial streetscape. Above it is a "proud and soaring thing."

The entry is pedestrian-friendly but undeniably elegant.

Lobbies feature touches of mid-century modernism which assure a certain timelessness.

The terrace between base and tower offers important amenities of a rental building.

The rooftop provides escape from the street and access to the skyline.

Thomas Jefferson designed the Rotunda at the University of Virginia, inspired by Palladio and by the Pantheon of Rome. Its beauty is deeply connected to its iconic familiarity and symbolic purpose.

Beauty

Seeking Harmony, Balance and Proportion

As Larry's ideas about architecture went deeper, and as he sought to identify and apply irreducible principles of design, his thinking circled around, in a way, to where he started. Early in his career, he took pleasure in pure geometry, assembling simple shapes to create complex designs. He was a sculptor as well as an architect as a young man, and he strove to create innovative and harmonious form.

Now, later in his career, the quest for harmony reemerged front and center, though this time it opened him to intuitive insights that reached to architecture's deepest wells. He was reading St. Augustine and Thomas Aquinas with new interest. Larry did not regard himself a philosopher and certainly not a theologian, but religious thinkers of the past had addressed architectural goals, inadvertently perhaps, but with surprising lucidity. "Beauty is the splendor of truth," is how Augustine reconciled the physical world with the spiritual one. In fact, sublime beauty in architecture would remain an elusive goal. But such thinking, Larry believed, could help an architect achieve ideal design by blending form, function, spirit and other elements with as much simplicity, or purity, as possible.

Truth comes from many sources. When Brunelleschi designed the Duomo of Florence he applied classical proportions which had been passed down over centuries. They were fused to his own entirely original engineering, worked out instinctively and without obvious precedent. Larry's reliable exemplar, Palladio, typically designed with a classical template and applied to it his own understanding of space and natural light. It was a rediscovery for the Renaissance and influenced architecture for centuries to come.

Larry understood that no one time or culture had a monopoly on beauty. The Christian philosophers had clarity as they provided practical, also familiar, architectural lessons as they additionally reinforced his religious faith. But many others had found the metaphysical in constructed objects. Louis Kahn contemplated a new design by asking "a brick… what it wants to be." Mies, a dedicated reader of St. Thomas, said "God is in the details." In Larry's case, he was convinced that he could distill architectural form to the point of essential and timeless character.

In 2018, Larry read *A Beautiful Question: Finding Nature's Deep Design*, by the physicist and Nobel Laureate Frank Wilczek who examined the question: Is the universe a work of art? Are principles of beauty hard-wired in nature? (Wilczek believes the answers to both questions are yes.) The physicist hypothesizes in his book that many forms of art, such as music and painting, have basic formulae in common that govern the physical world at large. He suggested that they apply no less to architecture.

As Larry read something of quantum physics he also surveyed

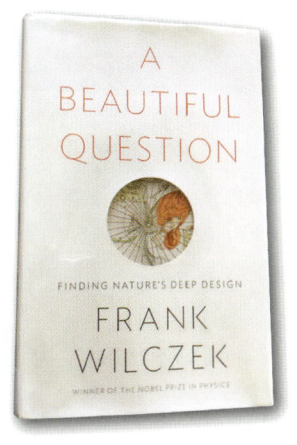

Wilczek's book examines the idea that beauty is the result of natural laws.

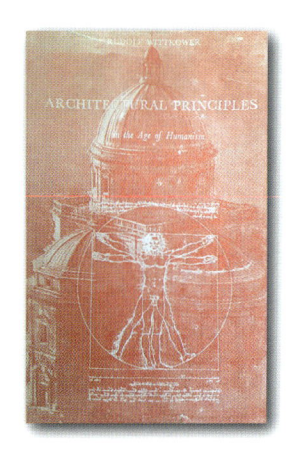

Wittkower's Architectural Principles in the Age of Humanism *discusses the absolute harmonies which were applied in the Renaissance.*

efforts of Greek philosophers. He concluded that beautiful constructions are those that mimic in some measure the phenomena of nature. Leonardo found classical proportions in the ideal human body. Frank Lloyd Wright reached back to the Froebel Blocks of his childhood for basic forms that
he, as a mature architect, assembled to achieve beautiful design. Le Corbusier had faith in the mathematical order of the universe and sought to capture it in architecture with the "golden section," which he regarded as "apparent to the eye and clear in their relations with one another."

How can architects apply these lessons? In fact, their training, classical or modern, and even without the mathematical precisions of the golden section, typically stresses attention to proportions that approximate it. For centuries they have sought the underlying harmonies found in successful architecture of the past. The modernists' frequent bias, ill-advised in Larry's view, was that they rejected history as a guide to the present.

While Larry admired the innovative rigor of modernism, he discerned early that despite its sparseness it had more in common with traditional architecture than many contemporaries admitted. This came to him vividly on a visit to Paris. He discovered, and not for the first time, that its architecture enjoys overall beauty and harmony, with classical buildings and modern ones exhibiting remarkable unity with one another.

Larry reasoned rightly that this success is the clear result of the Beaux-Arts tradition that has infused the city's architecture for centuries. Traditionally and especially in the Belle Époque, the Beaux-Arts system involved the *esquisse*, an intensely detailed collage with many elements of an integrated design—floor plan, elevation, ornament—when taken together reveal an essence. The *esquisse* harnessed the complexity of the Paris Opera. Less obviously, the principle guided the design of the Pyramid in the courtyard of the Louvre, as modernist I.M. Pei distilled and synthesized his faceted glass form to harmonize with the intricate geometry of the old museum.

It was not easy to achieve what was both simple and beautiful, nor to achieve beauty in the complex and elaborate. But both simple architecture and the complex draw from the same source. The phrase "form follows function" became the effective ally of mid-century modernism which promoted minimalism in trying to create buildings of machine age beauty. But "form ever follows function," as originally expressed by Louis Sullivan, was never meant to be mechanistic. Sullivan's architecture is functional but it is also emotional. His buildings tapped the poetic harmonies of nature from

Froebel Blocks taught Wright that complex form was assembled of simple elements.

the rusticated stone of the base around the exterior to the soaring weightlessness of the ornament above.

The lessons that Larry took and were absorbed by his firm are that this or any century's best architecture achieves the harmonies found in nature. That led him to replace the strict doctrines of the Bauhaus with an "architecture of humanism." This phrase he draws from the title of the book of 1914 by English author Geoffrey Scott who defended the depth of meaning and emotion in classical architecture, as even then it was disparaged by modernists.

Thus Larry's career has been a consistent effort to discover the most fundamental values of architecture and to use them. His understanding of those values led to the design approach that he transmits to his colleagues at Booth Hansen, and to students at Northwestern University where he teaches. By stressing the universal virtue of beauty, he identifies what is at once the simplest goal of architecture and the most complex to understand. In the best work of Booth Hansen, efficiency is only one aspect of a beautiful building. In Larry Booth's world, advanced architects recognize that the needs of structure and space are judged against their ability to touch the emotions that great architecture can affirm.

The Beaux-Arts esquisse *seeks harmony in all elements of a project, including its drawings.*

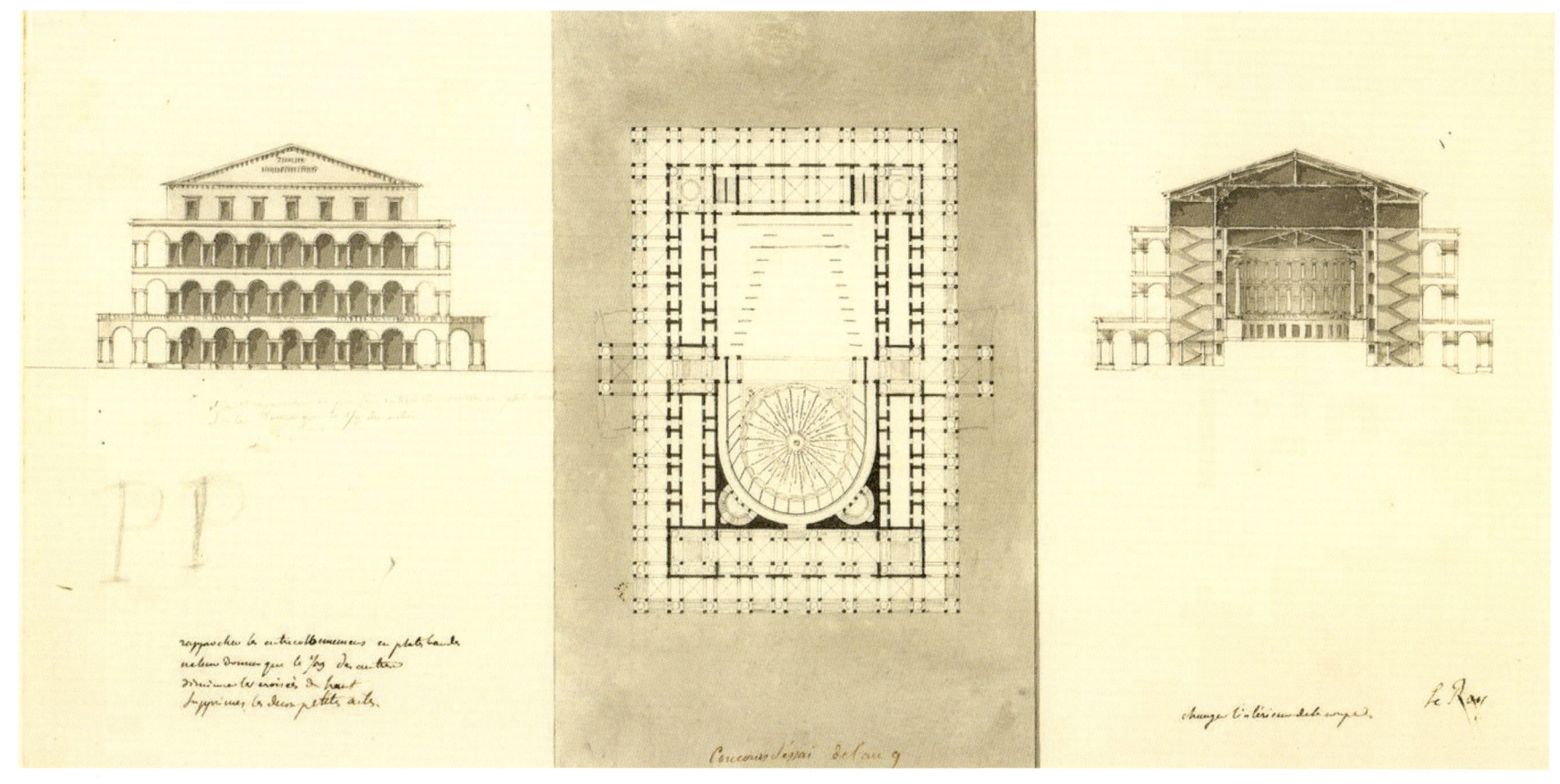

Chicago Botanic Garden
Plant Conservation Science Center
and Learning Center

Glencoe, Illinois, 2009, 2016

The Science Center is raised above a wetland on the edge of the property

At the Chicago Botanic Garden, two major Booth Hansen projects met the specific needs of science in one case, and education in the other. They also reflect the traditional architecture of the Garden which was designed originally in the 1960s, with contributions from modernists Edward Larrabee Barnes and Dan Kiley. From its beginnings the institution demonstrated that harmony between nature and the built environment is possible and sometimes sublime.

In the Plant Science Center, Booth Hansen raised the building on pylons over the wetland site on the edge of the Garden's property. Doing so left the watershed undisturbed, a key objective in suburban conservation, and it had the aesthetic benefit of encouraging sedges and other water-loving grasses to grow around the building's base. The simple *parti* has distinctly classical symmetry, and its double-high central space features clerestories which increase natural light and provide sightlines to rooftop gardens.

In this laboratory complex of the Chicago Botanic Garden, Booth Hansen started with critical performance benchmarks. The multi-use building would house workrooms for advanced scientific work. It would also directly serve the institution's mission as a museum, with the central space providing visual access to glassed-in labs and serving as an exhibit hall.

The building is complex but refined, the result of an orchestrated design team of many professionals. Green-architecture consultants worked at the front end of the project and introduced elements such as solar-control glass and sunshades laced with photovoltaics. In construction, creative contractors helped architects solve problems such as the composition of concrete flooring exposed to otherwise damaging winter temperatures from underneath the raised building. The result of this teamwork was architectural performance at the highest level.

The Learning Center likewise met an array of benchmarks in terms of functionality, sustainability and harmony with the environment. The landscape around the building features whimsical landforms, largely to attract children and introduce the Garden's message of "the power of plants to sustain and enrich life." The architecture has a low profile and elliptical floor plate which reinforce the idea that the building is bound to the earth.

Interior traffic patterns curve and cross through wide corridors, and the use of high-performance glass creates sightlines between indoor spaces, and to outdoor classrooms which fan out into the building's backyard. Many other elements of the architecture such as overhangs, solar panels and its south-facing orientation transmit the message that human contributions to the natural world can be beautiful and even dramatic.

Left: The central atrium space of the science center is lined with glass and views of laboratories.

Below: Gardens outside the laboratory building are organized to facilitate experimentation.

Right: The elliptical footprint of the Learning Center wraps around the main entry to the building.

Below: Landforms provide a transition from the vast gardens around the Learning Center to the classrooms inside.

The interior of exhibit spaces, glassy courtyards, and outdoor classrooms create a space of discovery and calm, qualities that the Botanic Garden features throughout its 400 acres and diverse programs.

Mohawk Street Residence

Chicago, 2008

Along with luxurious space and expensive finishes, any mansion, modern or otherwise, requires conscientious design to assure that the project is driven by an integrated set of ideas. This Chicago residence began with the client's desire for a place where the family could live in comfort, interacting with the city but also providing peaceful refuge from it.

In this case, Booth Hansen chose an Irish Georgian model, Georgian because it would harmonize with the historic streetscape, Irish because the Georgian style in Ireland was less extravagant than other models, aligning the house with the unpretentious neighborhood. The fact that the clients were Irish brought an additional element of emotion to the design.

The conventions of Georgian architecture are well-known in America. It transmits a measure of nobility. It is also a sign of comfort and connection with the past. Authentic character is achieved through careful proportion and subtle detail. Irish Georgian elements of this home include a centered entry and unadorned, slightly recessed windows. The buff brick is neutral in color, in deference to the Irish model and also to this once-working class neighborhood.

Georgian architecture enables lengthy sightlines from front to back and side to side. This amplifies the openness of the house and also organizes the floor plan to make the most of its space on what is an ample but not unlimited urban site. The relative simplicity of the interior is punctuated by focal points where the house can display luxurious elements. Extravagance is not exhibited in ornament but rather in the craftsmanship that created the sweeping staircase of the double-high foyer, for example, and the garden which offers visual respite from the otherwise densely populated North Side of Chicago.

The entry of the Mohawk Street House is luxurious for its materials, craftsmanship and the spaces in between.

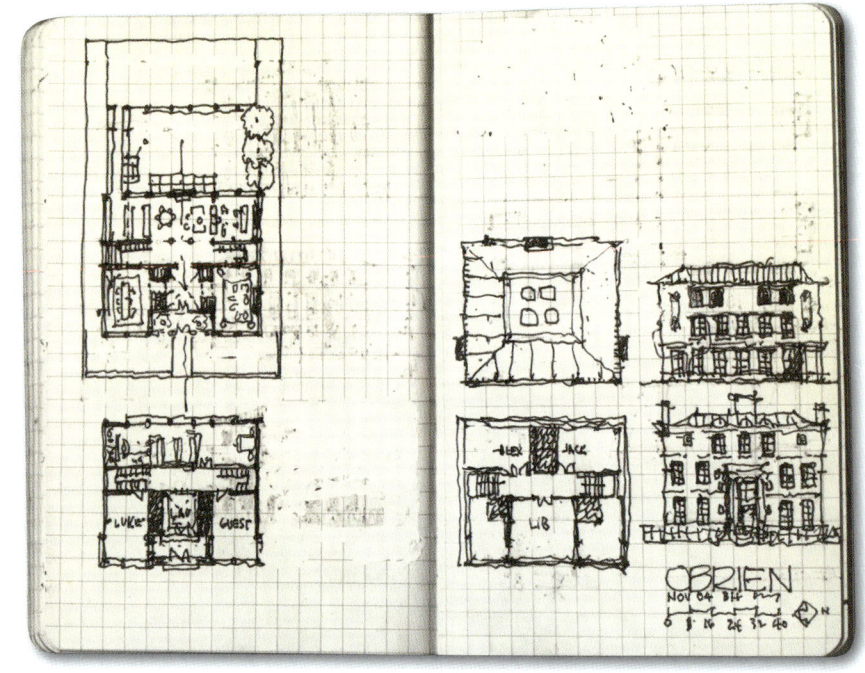

The beauty of the Irish Georgian resides in basic forms and proportions.

New Buffalo Residence

New Buffalo, Michigan, 2015

Traditional craftsmanship and sure proportions are highlighted in the New Buffalo Residence, conceived as four separate cedar-clad cottages linked by connecting volumes. On one end is the master bedroom, connected by a glassy breezeway to a space with a vaulted family room. A dining and entertainment space forms a connection to a third cottage, which is a genteel bunkhouse for an extended family. A shed completes the linear arrangement.

The house features the familiarity of vernacular form—the simple lines and materials of fishermen's cottages, evocative of Lake Michigan's shoreline which is within earshot through the wooded property. The 6,500 square-foot structure also involves the unembellished minimalism of the modern with the suggestion of a structure built incrementally over time.

The residence is designed for a client who wanted both intimacy and expansiveness. It also has a low-maintenance character with its shingle siding, metal roofs and sustainable zinc cladding on the connector spaces. This simple design is driven by the knowledge that certain forms and proportions are timeless, and that they are found in historic architecture as well as classic modernism. Both are equally responsible for a house that provides comfort and beauty.

While eminently refined, the house appears as a series of small structures designed and added as needed.

The New Buffalo Residence is a luxurious home, and spacious, which maintains a vernacular feel.

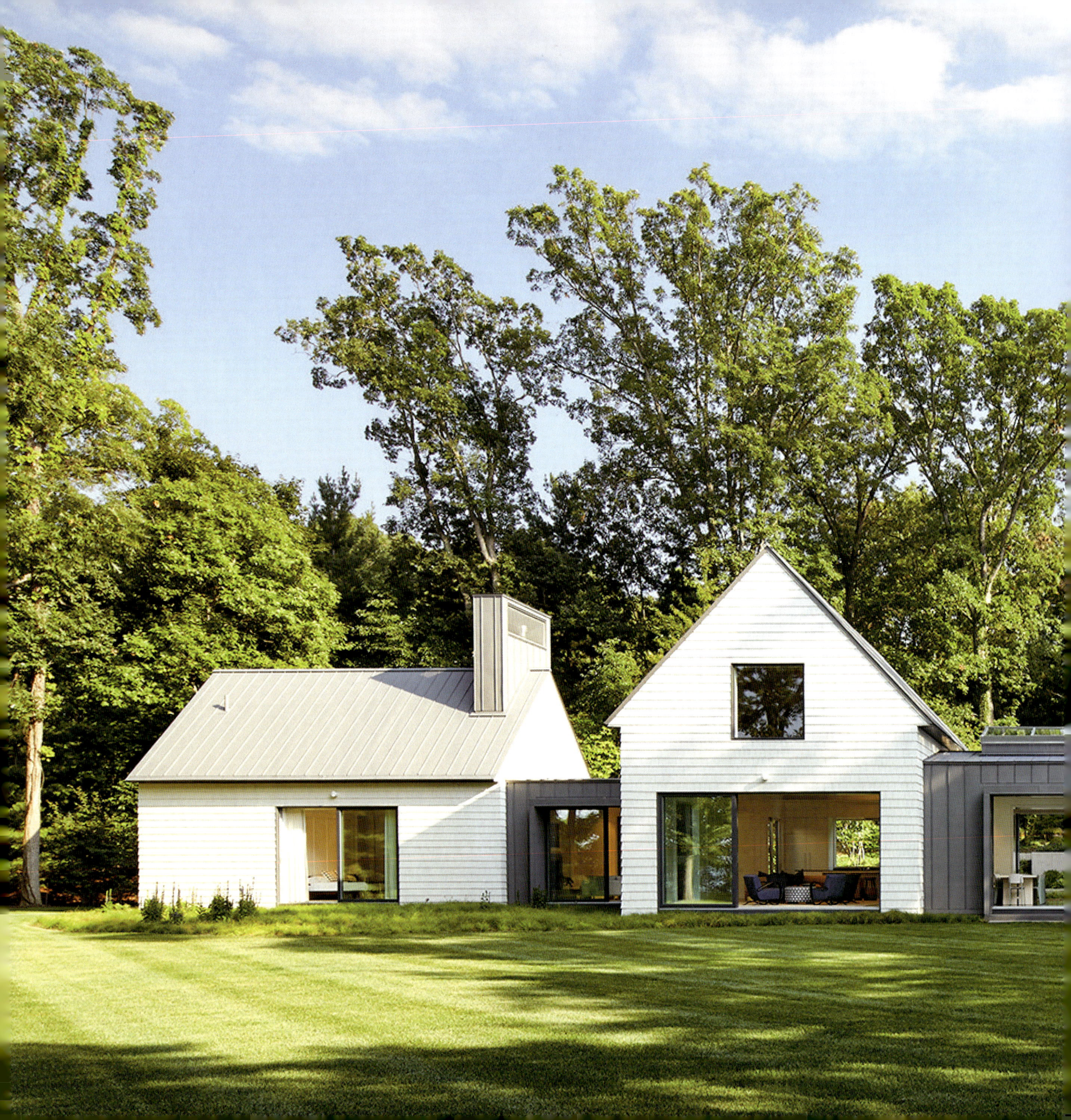

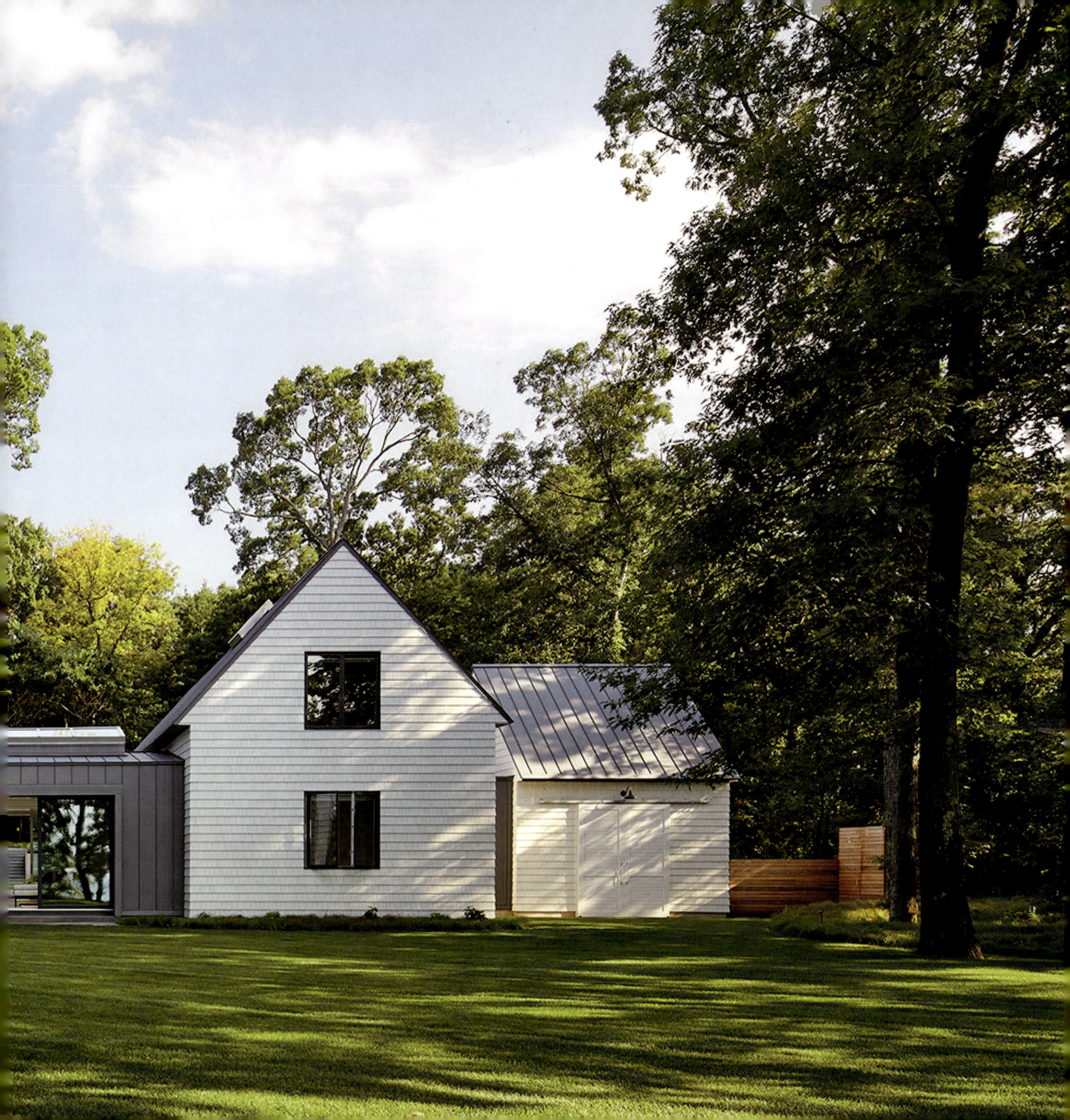

Shingle siding and tin roofs represent time-tested sustainability.

Sections are connected with passages and courtyards that expand living space outdoors.

Intimate spaces open extravagantly to the outside.

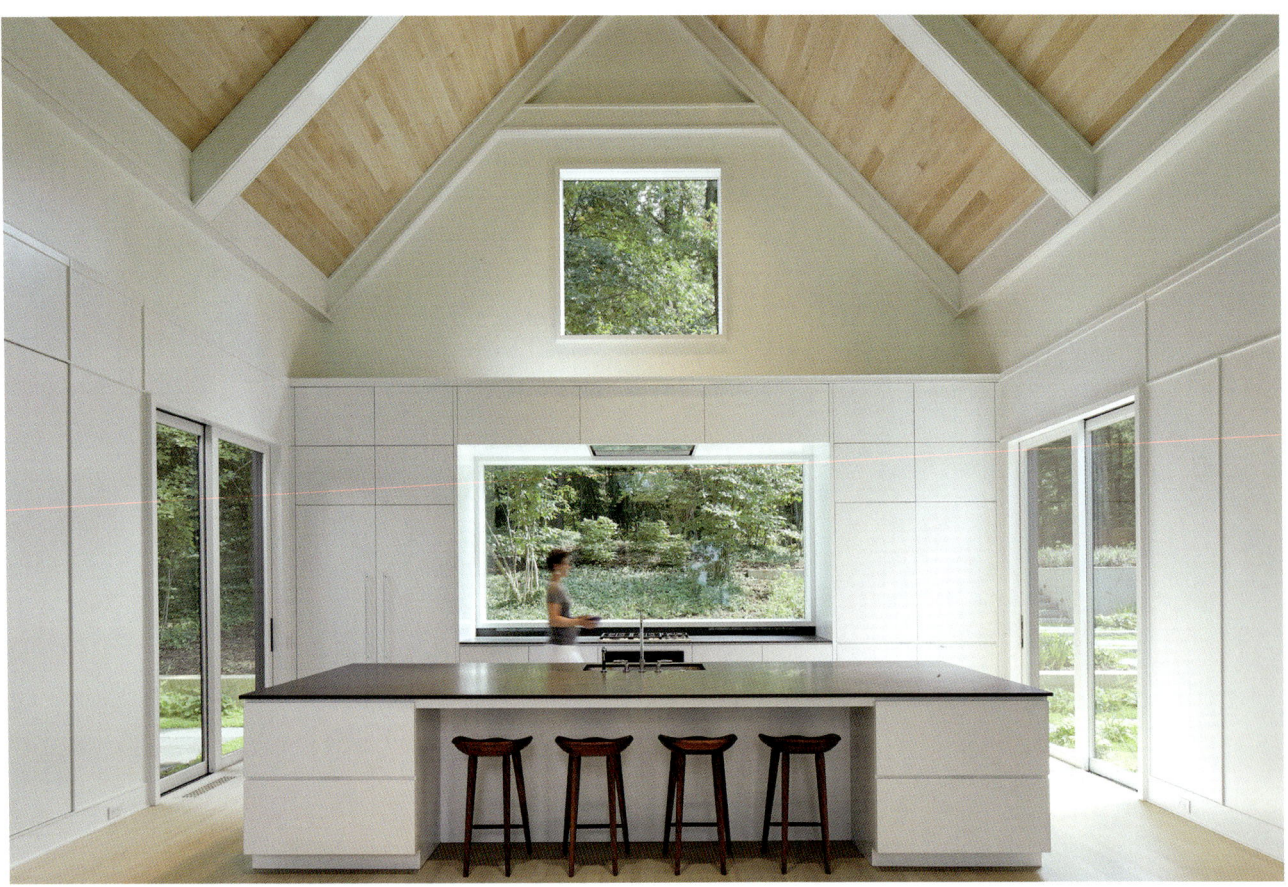

The geometry of the traditional house is emphasized and renders modernity, also simplicity.

Deming Place Condominiums

Chicago, 2015

The property is shallow, and the client required a design to maximize interior space and light.

The diversity of work from the Booth Hansen studio corresponds with the many varied sites presented to the firm by clients. The Deming Place neighborhood in Lincoln Park is an old one, though in continuous flux, and its architectural history is both traditional and modern. One objective of this project was to harmonize in scale with Victorian townhouses nearby and in form with larger, more modern buildings that have also gone up. For reasons related to zoning, the Deming Place building is a mid-rise of four-stories with a relatively long street presence of six long-span bays.

The scale is reduced on the street as the building's breadth is divided into two separate, identical sections, each with its own entry and elevator service. Its base and structural columns are revetted in smooth limestone, which is a reference to the neighborhood and especially the pre-world War II buildings of the neighborhood. Texture is rough in mullions and spandrels, providing a touch of hand craftsmanship as well as highlighting its structure.

Luxury was a prime necessity here, and it resides in the spaciousness of the units, some of them duplexed. Beginning at around 1,500 square feet and ranging to 3,000 square feet, layouts are flowing with interlocking space. Window walls in front and balconies in back fill the 9.5-foot-high living spaces with natural light and an open feel. The project affirms that what is valued today in multifamily buildings, aside from maximum comfort, is a street presence which is pedestrian-friendly to residents and to passersby.

Opposite page: The facade features gestures that suggest depth and emphasize spaciousness within.

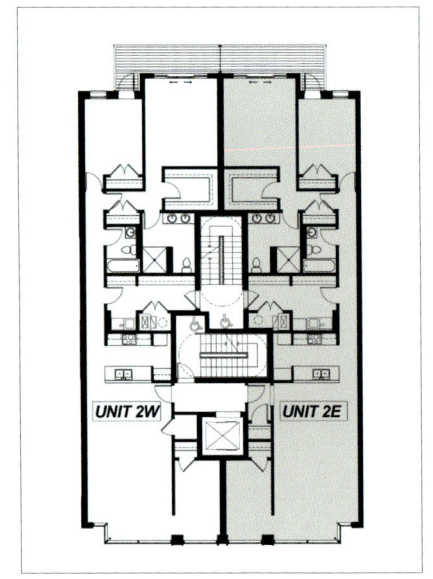

173

Palm 2150

Palm Springs, 2020

This development consists of 17 condominiums configured in a U-shape with the front door of each house facing inward. The layout encourages a communal spirit, with the central courtyard occupied by a swimming pool, landscaping and common areas for socializing. From the back, the houses have panoramic views of high plain and mountains. The design has a desert character with white stucco exterior walls, and also modernist horizontality, typical of Palm Springs.

Palm 2150 breaks new ground in Palm Springs in this less densely settled northeast portion of the city. Luxurious finishes are incorporated in efficient designs, with most layouts 17-feet-wide by 34-feet-long and largely open floor plans. First floors have living areas and master bedrooms, and most second floors have two additional bedrooms. Each townhouse has a private garden in back, with trellises providing shade for back yards that face south. Second-floor terraces are added on to the end units.

The interior courtyard provides for the main entries to the project's 17 townhouse condominiums. This feature encourages sociability while each unit also has a walled private garden in the rear.

Sited on the edge of the developed parts of Palm Springs, the design retains the feel of a desert oasis.

The pool, a common amenity and social center, dominates the entry courtyard.

The cool white that marks the interiors of the condominiums contrasts with colorful views outside.

The Chicken Coop, in Lake Bluff, on the prairie in the fall.

Permanence
Blending Timeless Values

Like many architectural practices, Booth Hansen has evolved as time has passed. This is natural for a lone practitioner or small firm, which was Larry's situation when he started and worked on commissions of modest scale. Larger firms, as Booth Hansen has become, change too, though ships of substantial size usually turn slowly.

What is remarkable about Booth Hansen is the way in which its leadership has continued to evolve even as its projects have become more expansive in scale and its design teams increasingly complex.

This has been accomplished through intense introspection on the part of Larry and the people who work closely with him. As a young man, Larry embarked on a process that involved the integration of many ideas, an impulse born of rigorous training and the will to defend his personal vision against the prevailing styles at the time.

In recent years, Booth Hansen has worked on a deeply collaborative basis, but has not abandoned its values. Larry has remained the firm's chief designer, but he is also involved in organizing design teams and getting the most out of their members, including architects, engineers, contractors, and not least, the client—essentially integrating their varied ideas and ability to contribute.

Larry's success in this respect is not unprecedented, but it is rare, and in Booth Hansen's case, it is an affirmation that architectural design does not stand still. As each commission is unique, ideas can and should shift as time passes and circumstances change. At the same time, Booth Hansen's work also expresses the timelessness that architecture achieves at its best, and does so by seeking and adhering to immutable values.

Early in his career, Larry's work was driven by the search for a *system*, as he called it, to guide his impulse to arrange simple forms into complex patterns. In this way, he found that he could achieve reason and clarity in his buildings. The ARCO service station, built in 1969, exemplified the effort to assemble basic elements into a series of functions.

Larry's fundamental objective has not changed. In the 2019 condominiums of 61 Banks Street, Chicago, the richness of the building is not only in its luxury—de rigueur on Chicago's Gold Coast—but in its visual order which harmonizes with the existing fabric of the neighborhood. Granted that the Banks Street project is a distinctly 21st century building, it blends seamlessly with much older nearby buildings by amplifying, not clashing with, the geometry of the neighborhood.

Larry's next step was to delineate or codify a *process* to assure

The Gold Coast's identity consists of high-rise apartments and limestone masonry, which new buildings in the area do well to reflect but not imitate.

that he and his team would achieve its objectives, every time, never twice the same. Integrating complex elements into successful architecture should not be left to the chance spark of inspiration. Larry's belief in an orderly method was driven also by the reality that architecture is deeply collaborative, and innovative design especially requires the organized input of many hands.

By the year 2000, Booth Hansen had achieved renown for an architecture which Larry characterized as modern beyond any one style. Its innovative approach drew easily from many sources, some modern and others traditional. What bound diverse elements together, they found, was an ineffable quality, their feel or *spirit*. He found that sensations of freedom, emotion and connection with nature represented the notes of spirit that could succeed in the blending of forms and functions.

The Glassberg House in Indiana represents an example of a discernible spirit. The minimalism of its glass walls and unadorned trim blend with the structure's enviable site, a primeval sand dune. Beyond the transparency of the house, its polished concrete floors inside and out appear as natural as the native grasses around the perimeter. Its undulating curved roof, the house's only elaborate feature, echoes the windswept character of the terrain on the edge of Lake Michigan.

As the 21st century progressed, Larry and Booth Hansen were at the top of their powers. Their ability to create buildings of simplicity and economy, as expected of the modern, and which were also infused with tradition, made Booth Hansen sought after by top clients in Chicago and elsewhere. And increasingly, his ability to achieve this signature was consistently achieved by transmitting his vision to the firm at large. Teamwork depends upon process,

An Indiana sand dune is gentle and even fragile, which its accompanying architecture must recognize.

Architecture at the Botanic Garden coexists with colorful canopies and rich texture.

as he knew, and its desired outcome is the highest standard of performance.

Years of thinking about this led him to Compass Points, not a roadmap but a series of fundamental principles, directly stated, that drive *total performance*. They are precepts that all team members can understand, discuss and share.

Simplicity is one criterion. Stewardship of the environment is another. Two major buildings at the Chicago Botanic Garden were strongly guided by Compass Points. Its tenets of performance facilitated interaction between architects, consultants, contractors and everyone else who might be tasked to solve a problem.

As Booth Hansen's ideas matured, they sought to understand the ultimate reward of architecture, which they recognized as *beauty*, which is achieved in so many cases by simplicity. While the practice came to involve larger structures, their skills enabled them to reduce complexity to its beautiful essence.

An example is Booth Hansen's New Buffalo Residence, the succession of cottage-like structures connected with one another to create a spacious house in the country. It is proportioned to fit comfortably in a glade not far from a bluff over Lake Michigan. It is profiled to harmonize with mature oaks all around. Equally important, it inspires memories of farm houses and even the shingled fishermen's shacks that line many coastlines and shorelines.

While beauty is an irreducible value of Booth Hansen architecture, its truest test is in its look, feel and reality of *permanence*—as in the Usher House in Palm Springs. This one is a largely transparent structure of a minimal frame and high-performance glass. Its openness and connection with the desert is bracing. Its harmonies with nature appear as inevitable as the agelessness of the boulders that punctuate its site.

For Larry, finding the harmonies of nature in architecture, and vice versa, has been a career-long quest. When Booth Hansen produces work which they regard as successful, or perhaps even sublime, they know that it was achieved not by good fortune or the spark of unexpected genius, rather by the understanding of values that do not change in architecture. Larry's career has evolved with the discovery of guideposts which transcended whatever battle of styles is being fought at the moment.

This places Larry Booth and Booth Hansen among 21st century architects whose value-laden work makes promises of sustainability, stewardship, community and other social responsibilities. Larry, for one, meets the commitments by touching the insights of an architectural past that remain an indispensable, if sometimes invisible, part of the future.

The desert has elements of permanence, others of evanescence. Its best architecture reflects both.

Kohl-Feinerman House

Winnetka, Illinois, 2004

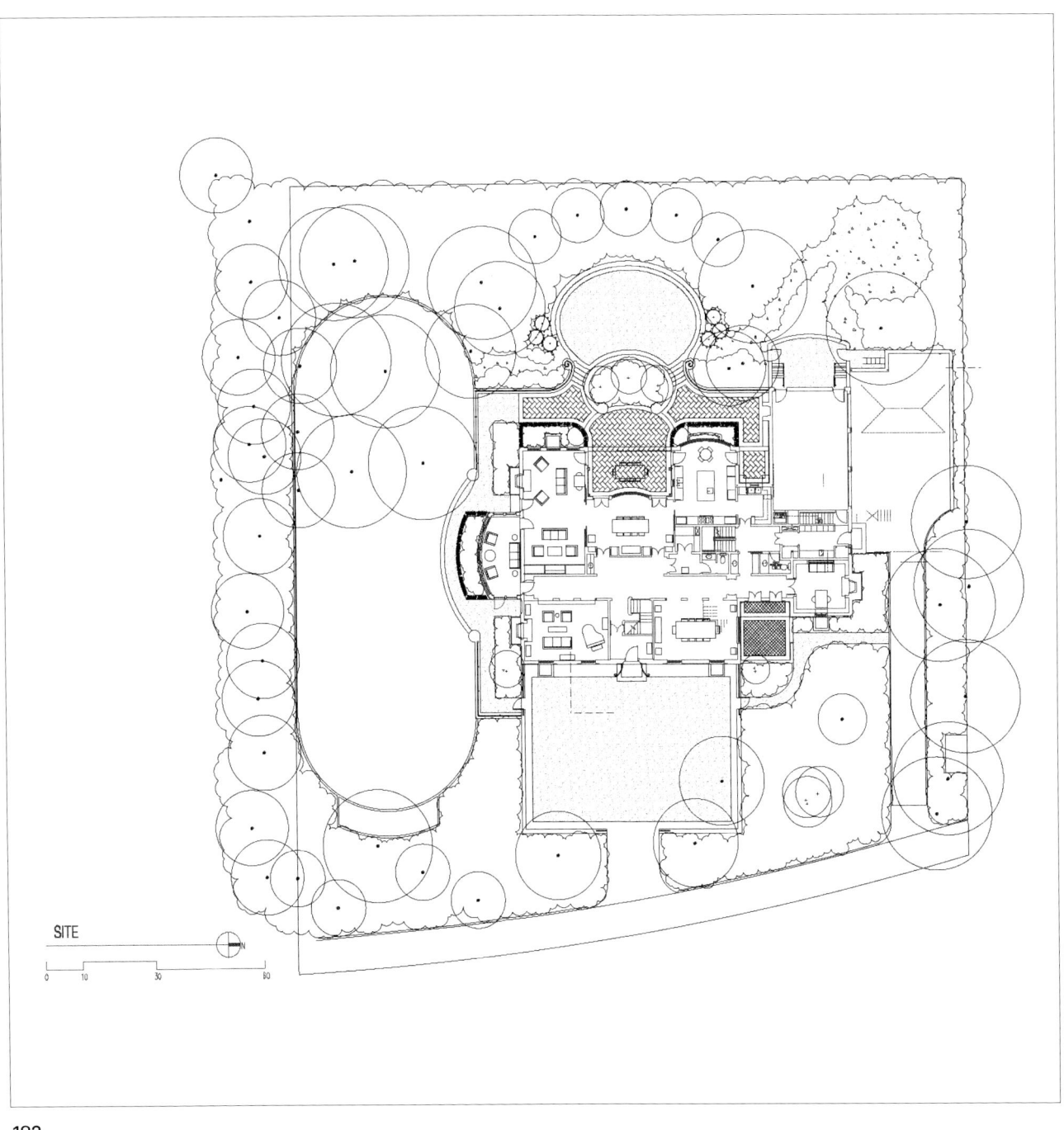

From the outside, the Kohl-Feinerman House in Winnetka has a distinctly traditional look, but it was designed largely from the inside out. The process involved the creation of large spaces for the family. Access to natural light also was a key factor, as was fine interior detailing with the overall muted tones of a country home. The flow between spaces and ultimately to the outside called for a strong axial floor plan.

The architectural vocabulary of this home's environs in Winnetka suggested the historically inspired exterior, while it also came into harmony with the interior. Notes of the French Provincial were appropriate with its large vertical windows (scaled like French doors), a hipped roof, arched dormers, and most of all its simplicity. Aspects of this essentially rural style were invented in centuries past when architects developed home designs, even for wealthy clients, from the simple template of agricultural buildings. The Kohl-Feinerman House is in no way agricultural, but nor is it excessively palatial.

This page and opposite: The Kohl-Feinerman House occupies a richly planted site in a suburb where traditional architecture shares a starring role with a few contemporary neighbors.

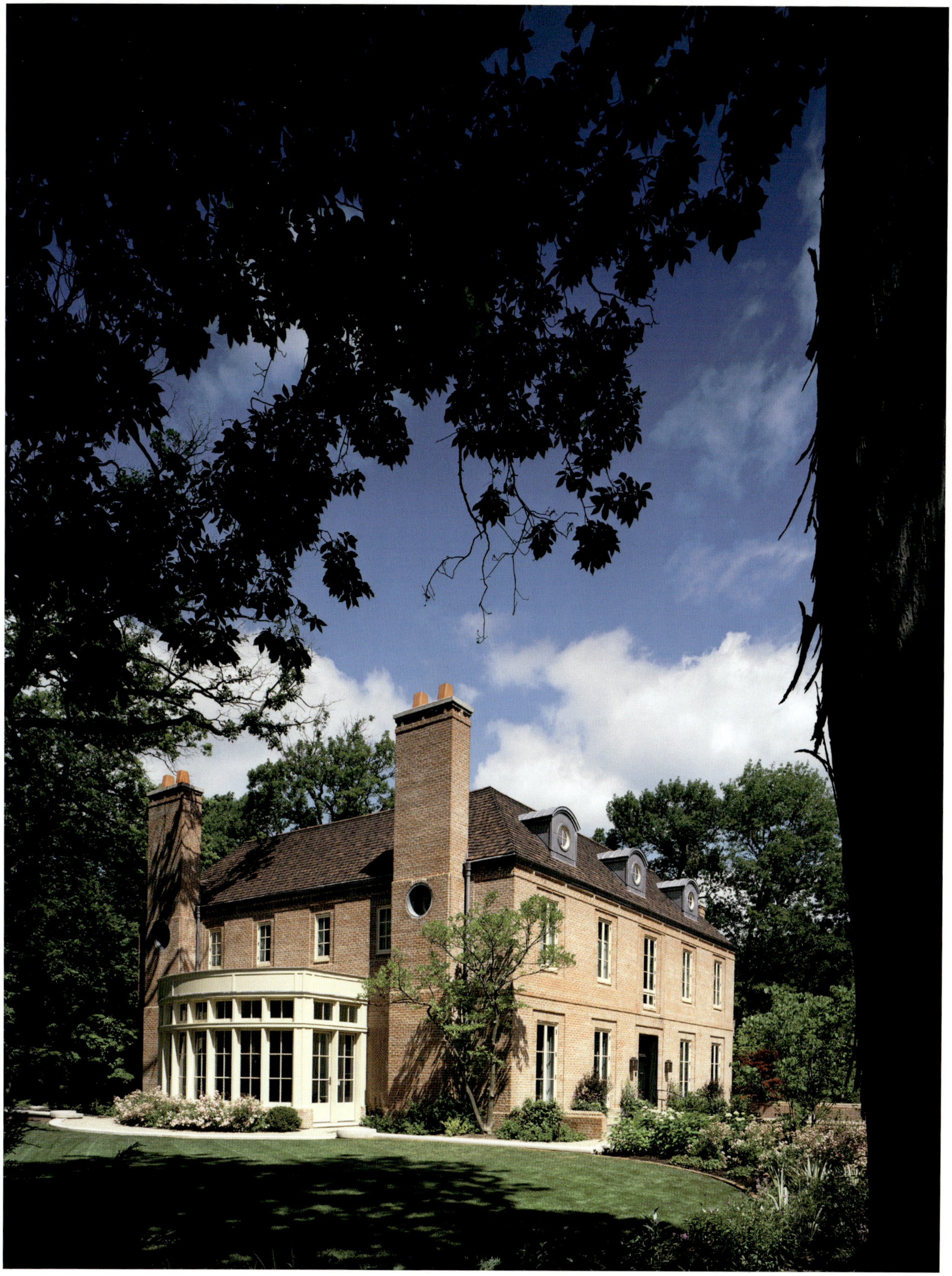

The traditional country house can be simplified while also retaining its classical proportions. Booth Hansen achieved simplicity and modernity in the house by stripping the exterior to its essentials.

Interior space flows to the patio and garden in back.

Glassberg House

Beverly Shores, Indiana, 2012

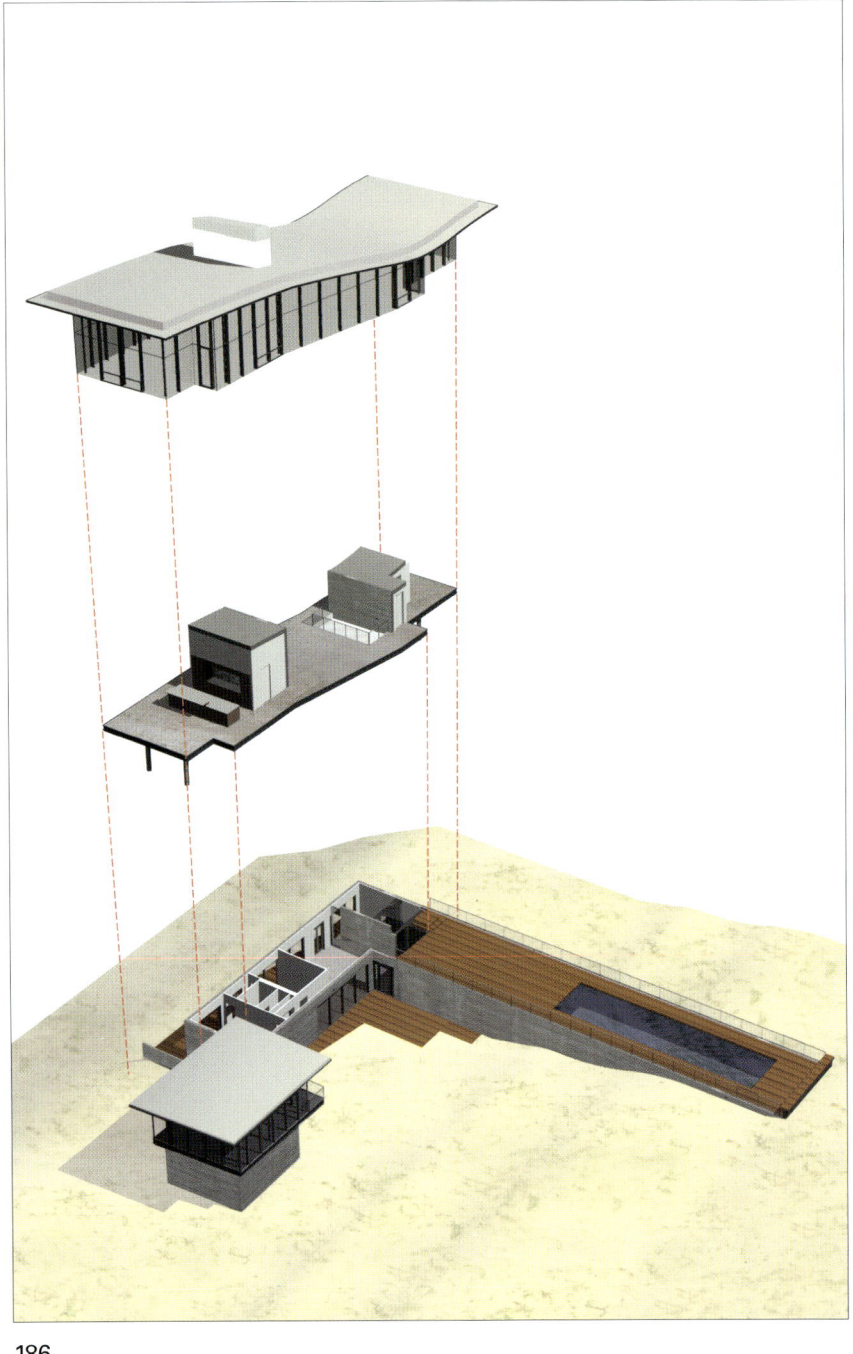

The Glassberg House occupies a primeval sand dune on the edge of Lake Michigan with architecture designed to highlight the site in a way that is less dramatic than it is sublime. Its most notable feature is transparency which permits views in all directions of the native flora around the perimeter and of the lake below.

What is detectible on close inspection is the craftsmanship of the construction, including the undulating roof which reflects the windswept terrain, finely milled lathing of unstained wood, and rough cut limestone inside and out. A pool and garden were designed to appear as links between the house and the natural landscape.

Another feature which is striking on second or third glance is the raw concrete flooring that extends around the outside perimeter and into the living spaces. The concrete floor achieves durability for the exterior and a fine finish suitable to the interior, where it is punctuated by colorful handmade rugs and discreetly positioned pieces of furniture. The concrete was a challenge that required an innovative solution for curing the surface which tapped the contractor's creativity as well as the architects'.

Opposite page: The simplicity of the Glassberg House required a high level of craftsmanship to achieve the elegance that the site deserved. The house is prominent on its site but scaled not to overwhelm it.

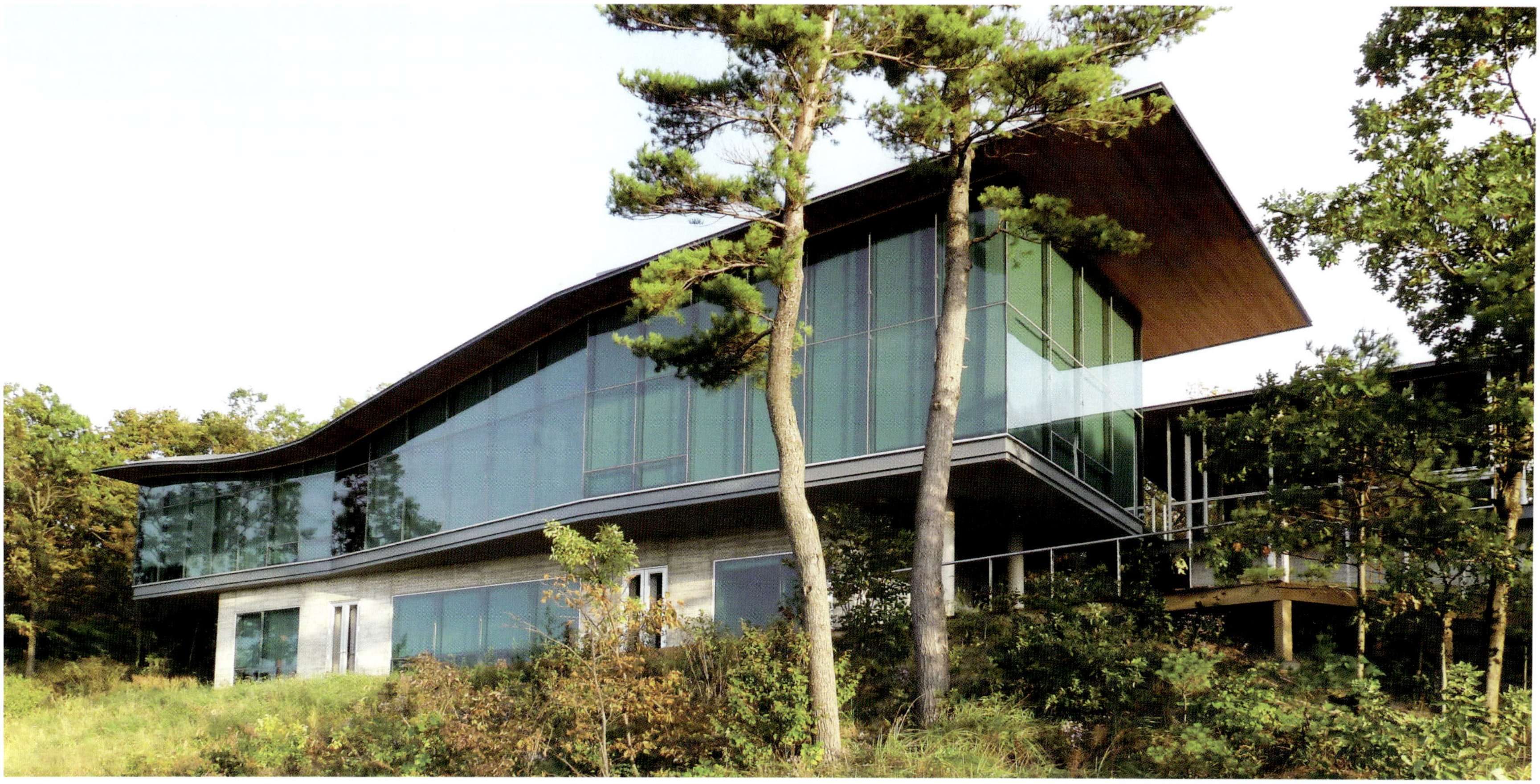

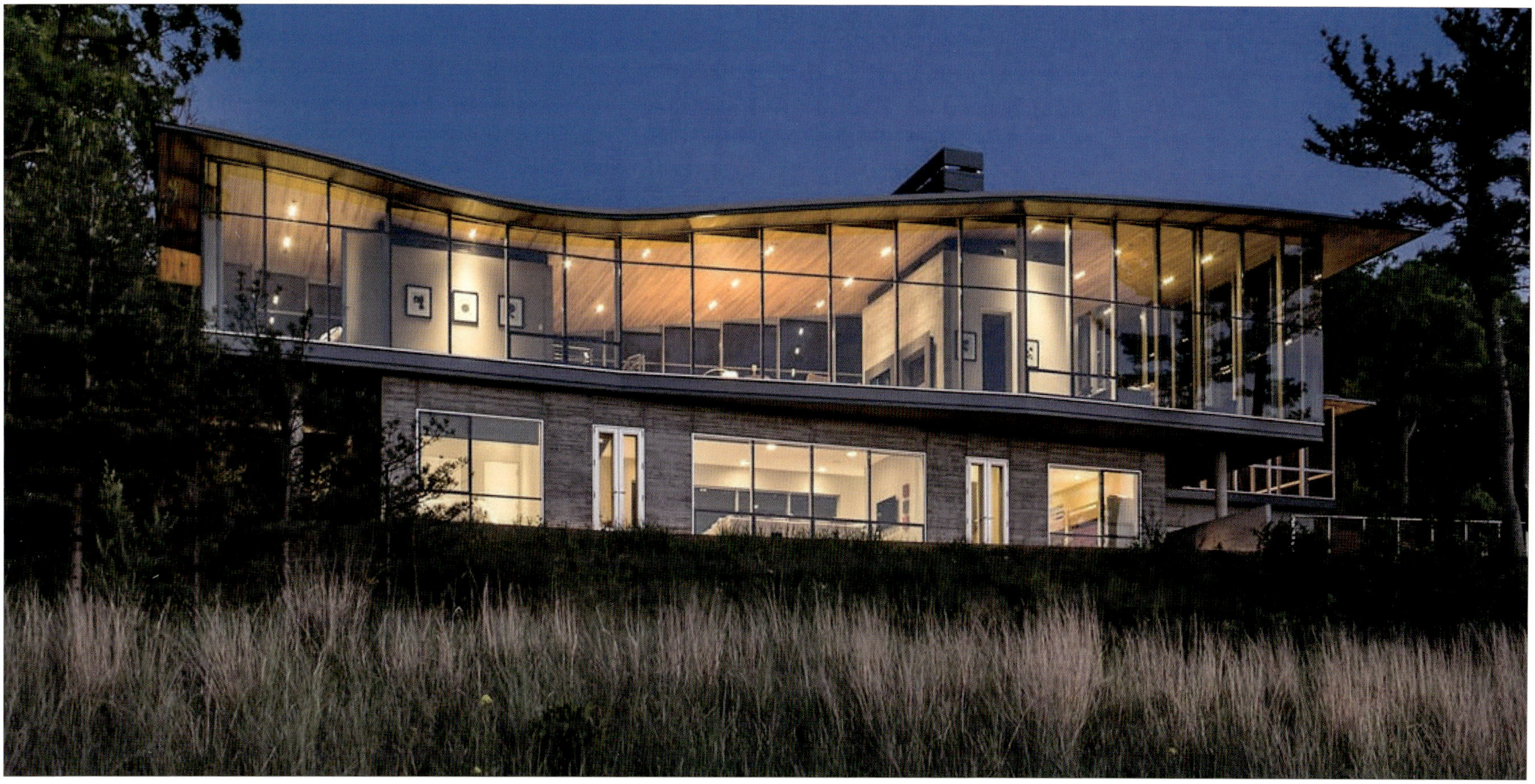

Discreet, if intense, excavation set the house comfortably on its sand dune.

Openness throughout the interior assures views of the beach and the lake.

Usher House
Palm Springs, 2016

The Usher House, a 5,000 square-foot contemporary home on a naturalized desert site, restores the precision and sense of proportion that guided classic mid-century modernism. This house is on the edge of the site of the Frederick Loewe Estate, built in 1956 for the composer.

The Booth Hansen design, which distills the essence of classic modernism, is of unbroken space and palette of basic materials. It began with the idea that the house should celebrate the site, which is a desert setting landscaped with boulders, succulent plants and long views of the dry plain and mountains. The house also required space for art and specifically a wall to accommodate a 42-foot-long painting which the client wanted prominently displayed.

While the rectilinear structure contrasts with the environs, it is comfortably settled into it. An expansive patio, an "infinity" pool and glassy one-story elevations harmonize with the terrain. Views from strategic points inside provide panoramas of a valley reaching into the remote distance.

While luxurious and visually dramatic, the design functions with simplicity and substantial sustainability. The floor plan is essentially a symmetrical cross pattern with a grand kitchen as its center point. Glass in all directions is of high-performance quality, and operable windows enable natural ventilation through clear span spaces. A strategy of passive solar design and photovoltaics reduce energy usage.

Despite the Usher House's innovative construction and mechanical systems, they are largely used as a means to eliminate unnecessary design elements. An example is the thin-profile windows, fabricated by a local specialty manufacturer. They open without visible hardware which would otherwise break up expanses of glass. This and other details contribute to a new relationship between efficient function and the objective of increasingly invisible form.

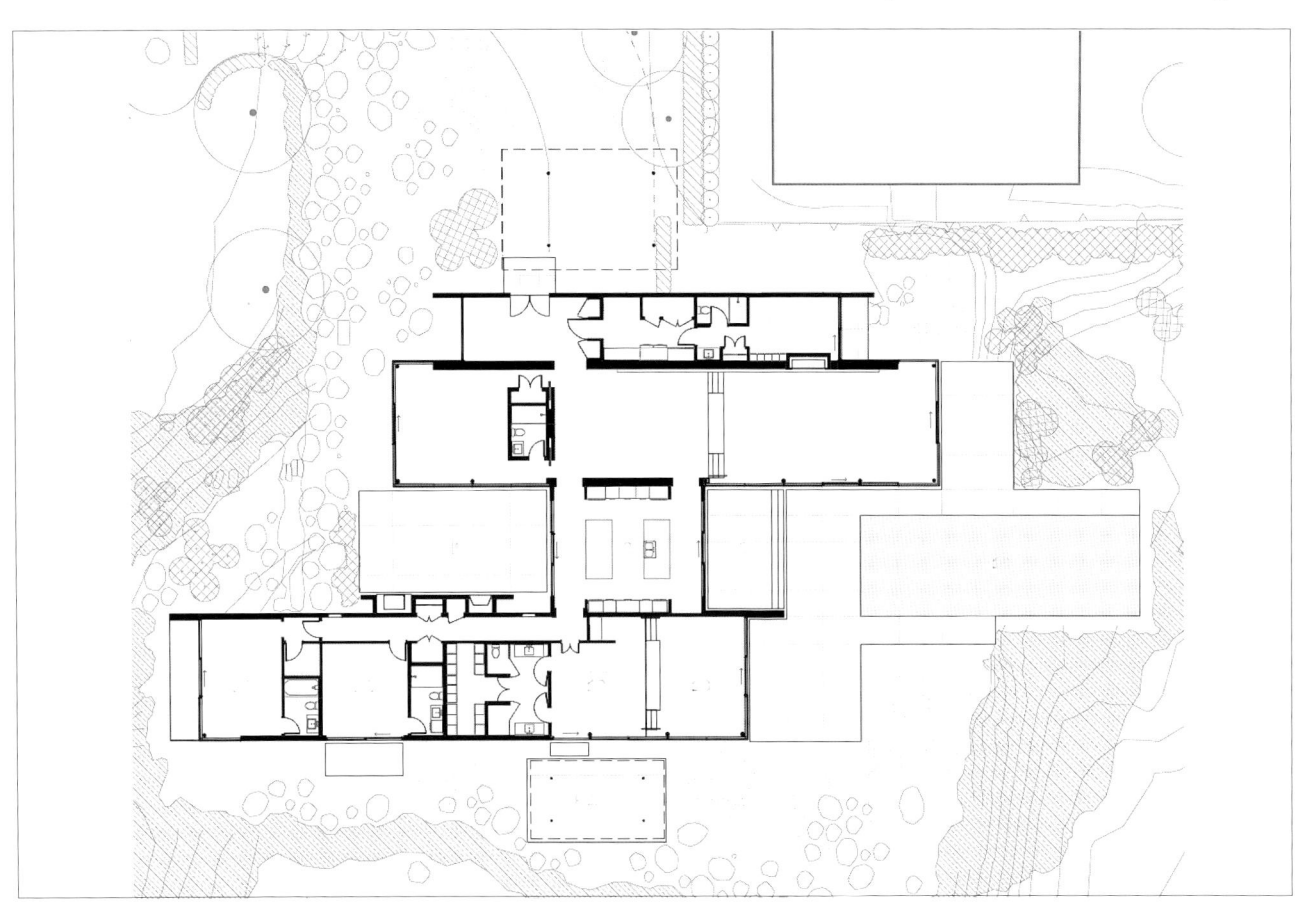

With two discernible axes connecting in the middle, rooms are organized to cluster spaces for sleeping, living, entertaining and other functions. Most have elaborate views and ready access to the outside.

The landscape is naturalized with boulders and brush to emphasize the roughness of the desert and its contrast with the house at the top of its gentle rise.

Modernism at it best celebrates the environment around it. It introduces a sense of proportion. It emphasizes color. It provides beautiful views. And it transmits the message that the compositions of nature, seemingly at random, are part of a larger order.

The angular planes of the structure represent a counterpoint to the organic form of the site.

The universal space inherent in modern architecture is amplified in the desert.

The house, the rock garden and the landforms beyond are starkly demarcated from one another, but they are parts of a natural composition.

The flow of the Usher House moves easily from space to space, creating a sense of comfort while also emphasizing the vastness of the environment.

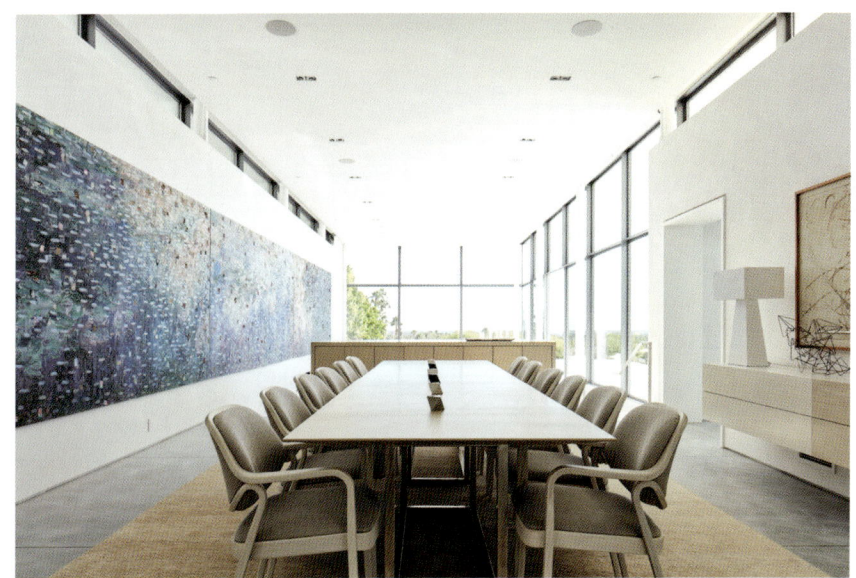

While the house offers dramatic panoramas, many views are layered and involve interior and exterior space together.

The house is on precisely ordered Cartesian axes. This enables the complexity of the place to create a certain mystery, especially at night, which is enchanting, never disorienting.

61 East Banks Street Condominiums

Chicago, 2019

The condominiums of 61 East Banks were designed to be relatively low to the ground, but with verticality and materiality harmonious with older tall buildings around it.

As the Gold Coast of Chicago continues to develop, a new building such as 61 East Banks requires attention to historical as well as modern functional elements, to take its place in one of the city's oldest and most desirable neighborhoods. The massing of this building, clad in masonry the color of limestone, is flattened like the Art Deco high rises of the pre-war neighborhood. Elevations on four sides are punctuated with minimally constructed metal-frame bay windows, a feature inspired by early 20th century modernism. The composition of the cladding and bays makes this rental apartment building a harmonious neighbor on its stretch of the lakefront. The unique blend of historic notes creates a building that is respectful of the neighborhood's distinguished past and contemporary in its refinement.

The design also incorporates a variety of less visible considerations. For one, the program required a variety of apartment sizes, of one, two and three bedrooms, and these are laid out to optimize interior space and views of the lake just across Lake Shore Drive. All layouts include large living rooms with projecting bays that amplify the sense of space and light.

Large bay windows punctuate the masonry walls and provide a sense of light-filled grandeur in the living spaces within.

The entry features a blend of glass-and-steel modernity and the tradition of well-wrought masonry.

The lobby appears timeless with wood paneling and limestone, but composed in ways that are unique and deceptively modern.

Daxton Hotel
Birmingham, Michigan, 2021

The Daxton constitutes a mildly classical gesture on the edge of downtown Birmingham.

For a hotel of distinction on a suburban site outside of Detroit, Booth Hansen mediated between the pedestrian scale of Birmingham's shopping district and a measure of monumentality at the edge of this village-like town center. While architects sometimes resist the idea of direct antecedents, the Daxton Hotel evokes the classical modernism that marks another nearby building, the Cranbrook Academy of Art by Eliel Saarinen.

Saarinen proved that classical architecture has the versatility to perform modern functions, in his case education, as Larry and Booth Hansen architect Scott Cyphers demonstrate here for a high-end hotel. Classical proportion enables a variety of design objectives. Its large vertical windows fill the interior with light. The template permitted the breaking down of scale for the structure to fit in more suitably on the existing streetscape, also the dissolving of the corners achieved with modern glazing. The building's simple division into blocks enables setbacks that create a green-roof over the ground floor and terraces outside luxury suites above.

Many architectural gestures of the hotel are subtle. Much of its luxury is in materiality—high-polish granite, black terrazzo, low-iron glass that enhances transparency inside and out. A ballroom's extravagantly clear-span space depends upon load transfer to an adjacent arcade, which itself creates dramatic procession of space. Outside, the lower stories are clad in slate-colored cast stone assembled with a handmade look.

The elegance of the place also depended upon teamwork with the hotel's interior designer and lighting contractor among others whose delicate touch helped create sensations that feel larger than the hotel's size on the quiet suburban site.

The hotel has a monumentality which is broken down in scale to fit comfortably into the suburban context.

Arcade on the hotel's first floor was engineered for significant load-bearing responsibilities.

The bar, ballroom and guest rooms were designed for spaciousness and intimacy by KTGY Simeone Deary Design Group, of Chicago.

205

St. Joseph Island Residence
Ontario, Canada, 2021

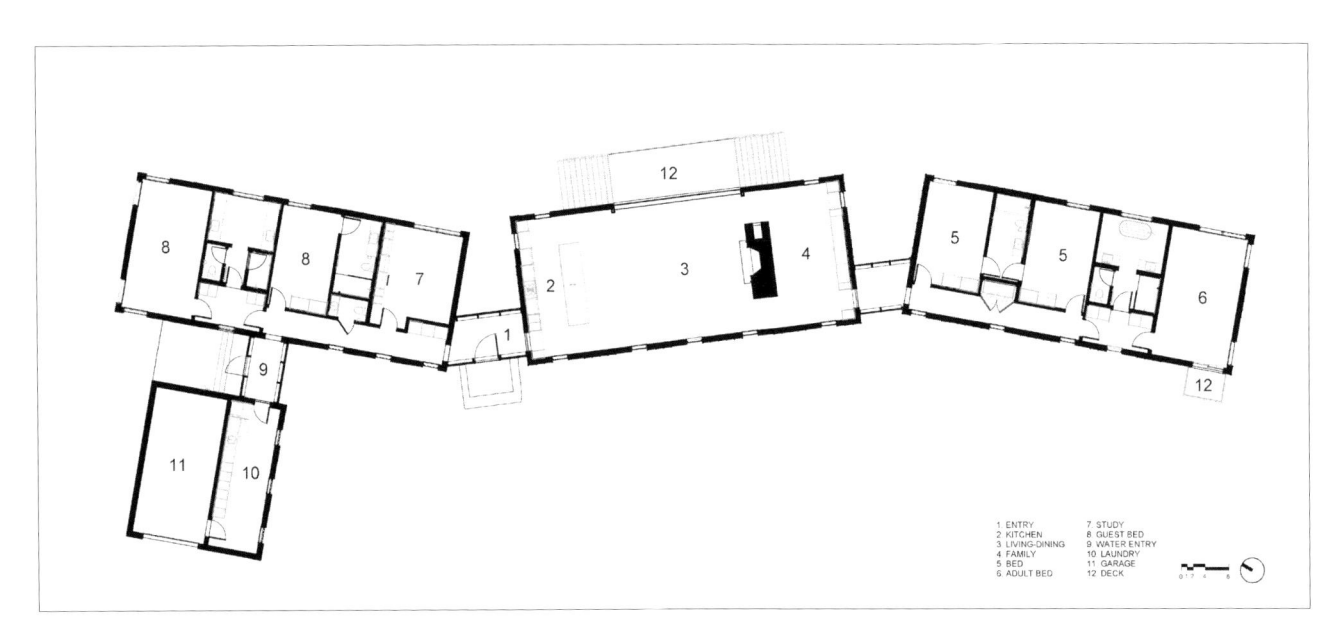

St. Joseph Island, Ontario, occupies a still-pristine corner of northern Lake Huron, and its natural beauty encouraged a high level of sustainability, not to mention the light touch of this vacation home's design. Visually, the dark, relatively low profile of the 4,500 square foot house (including detached studio) intrudes minimally on the backdrop of dark pines. Its three main sections are set irregularly to follow the line of the stony shore, while the subtle cant of their sitings also make the most of panoramic views from inside. The sections of the house, some with cathedral ceilings, are connected with glassy breezeways and aligned to enhance spacious interiors.

Zinc siding and roofing—bereft of eaves—create a profile of unbroken lines, a contemporary touch that also echoes the barns and fishing cabins of the historical environment. Zinc cladding, rated to last several decades without significant maintenance (it is also eminently recyclable) is a recently evolved material that old-time craftsmen might have used if they were building today. Also encouraging longevity as well as protection of the environment is the raised-pier foundation which enables unimpeded run-off of rainwater and snow melt.

The house adapts timeless gestures to achieve sustainability, such as the placement of windows for cross-ventilation, also in the peaks of gabled volumes to remove stack-effect heat in the summer. Modern insulation in the walls and floors of the structure accompanies geothermal loops for heating and cooling, which are run to the lake bed to stabilize high and low seasonal temperatures. Thus an area that was once largely a summer resort becomes comfortable all year long.

1. ENTRY
2. KITCHEN
3. LIVING-DINING
4. FAMILY
5. BED
6. ADULT BED
7. STUDY
8. GUEST BED
9. WATER ENTRY
10. LAUNDRY
11. GARAGE
12. DECK

Drawings illustrate the flow of the spacious interior, and how the construction would sit quietly on its wooded lake shore site.

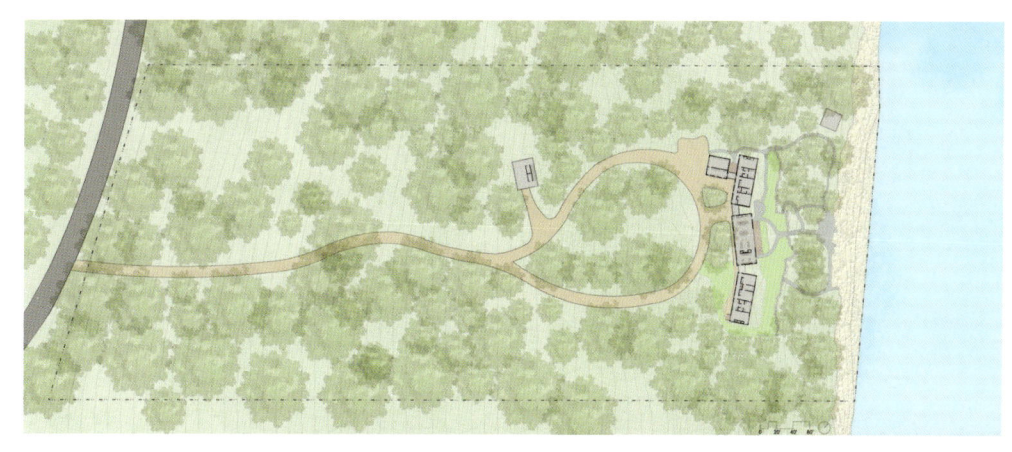

The house's footprint is canted, corresponding to the landscape's natural features.

207

The St. Joseph Island house has a modernity born of the proportions of historic structures that did once, and still, populate this corner of the North Woods.

Zinc cladding system involves sliding shutters that protect the house when occupants are absent. The relatively luxurious interior appointments include distinct splashes of color.

The isolation of the house is relieved by evening light and inviting interior features.

Deeper in the woods are the garage and a dance studio.

211

Image Credits

p. 2 Greg Murphey
p. 8 Nathan Kirkman
p. 12 Chicagogeek
p. 13 (top) Ken Lund
p. 13 (bottom right) Verner Reed
p. 14 Courtesy of MIT
p. 16 Orlando R. Cabanban
p. 17 Booth family
p. 18 Booth family
p. 19 (left) Booth family
p. 19 (right) Courtesy of Art Institute of Chicago
p. 20 (top) Courtesy of Stuart Cohen
p. 20 (bottom) Courtesy of Art Institute of Chicago
p. 21 Courtesy of Art Institute of Chicago
pp. 22, 23 Booth Hansen
p. 24 Booth Hansen
p. 25 Hedrich Blessing
p. 26 (drawing) Booth Hansen
pp. 26, 27 (photos) Philip Turner
pp. 28, 29 Orlando R. Cabanban
p. 30 (drawings) Booth Hansen
pp. 30, 31 Philip Turner
p. 32 (drawing) Booth Hansen
pp. 32, 33 (photos) Christian Staub
p. 34 Booth Hansen
p. 35 Michelle Litvin
p. 36 (drawing) Booth Hansen
pp. 36, 37 (photos) Orlando R. Cabanban
p. 38 Booth Hansen
p. 39 Joe Karr
p. 40 (top) Booth Hansen
p. 40 (bottom) From Rand, McNally & Co.'s *Bird's-eye views and Guide to Chicago*
p. 41 (right) *Architectural Digest*
p. 41 (bottom) Courtesy of Skidmore Owings & Merrill
pp. 42-45 Tony Soluri
pp. 46-49 Paul Worchol
p. 50 Booth Hansen
pp. 51-57 Michelle Litvin
p. 58 Booth Hansen
pp. 59-61 Timothy Hursley
p. 62 Gilbert Gorski
pp. 63-64 Booth Hansen
p. 65 Timothy Hursley
p. 66 Gloria Groom
p. 69 Booth Hansen
p. 70 (drawing) Booth Hansen
pp. 70-73 (photos) Timothy Hursley
p. 74 (drawings) Booth Hansen
pp. 74, 75 (photos) George Lambros

pp. 76, 77 (photos) Tim Hursley
p. 77 (drawing) Booth Hansen
p. 78 (drawing) Booth Hansen
pp. 79-81 Tim Hursley
pp. 82, 83 Bruce Van Inwegen
pp. 84, 86 (drawings) Booth Hansen
pp. 84 (photo) Greg Murphey
p. 85 (top) The Book of Kells
p. 85 (bottom) Greg Murphey
pp. 86, 87 (photos) Greg Murphey
pp. 88, 89 Booth Hansen
p. 90 (drawing) Booth Hansen
pp. 90, 91 (photos) Bruce Van Inwegen
p. 92 Wayne Cable
p. 93 (drawings) Booth Hansen
pp. 93-97 (photos) Wayne Cable
p. 98 Courtesy of Chicago History Museum
pp. 99-101 (photos) Greg Murphey
pp. 100, 101 (drawings) Booth Hansen
p. 102 (drawing) Booth Hansen
pp. 102, 103 (photos) Claudio Santini
p. 104 Booth Hansen
p. 105 Greg Murphey
pp. 106, 107 Michelle Litvin
p. 108 (drawing) Booth Hansen
pp. 108-111 (photos) Michelle Litvin
pp. 112-115 Booth Hansen
p. 116 (drawing) Booth Hansen
p. 116 Brian Fritz
pp. 117-119 Greg Murphey
pp. 120, 121 Hedrich Blessing
p. 122 (drawing) Booth Hansen
pp. 122, 123 (photos) Hedrich Blessing
pp. 124-127 Mark Ballogg
p. 128 (top) Courtesy of Joffrey Ballet
p. 128 (bottom) Michelle Litvin
p. 129 Michelle Litvin
pp. 130, 131 Steve Hall
pp. 132-135 Mark Ballogg
p. 133 (drawing) Booth Hansen
p. 134 Michelle Litvin
p. 135 (top) Mark Ballogg
p. 135 (bottom) Michelle Litvin
pp. 136, 137 Michelle Litvin
pp. 138-141 Wayne Cable
p. 141 (drawing) Booth Hansen
pp. 142, 143 Booth Hansen
p. 144 Steve Hall
p. 145 (left) Hedrich Blessing
p. 145 (right, top) Courtesy of Chicago History Museum

p. 145 (right, bottom) Steve Hall
pp. 146, 147 Jon Miller
p. 148 Booth Hansen
pp. 149-153 Dave Burk
p. 154 Bestbudbrian
p. 155 Courtesy of Penguin Group
p. 156 Courtesy of Seth Kaller
p. 157 Booth Family
p. 158 Michelle Litvin
p. 159 (top photos) Michelle Litvin
p. 159 (bottom) Chicago Botanic Garden
p. 160 (top) Chicago Botanic Garden
p. 160 (middle and bottom) Steve Hall
p. 161 Steve Hall
p. 162 (photo) Michelle Litvin
p. 162 (drawing) Booth Hansen
p. 163 Bruce Van Inwegen
pp. 164-171 Steve Hall
p. 172 (photo) Michelle Litvin
p. 172 (drawing) Booth Hansen
p. 173 Booth Hansen
p. 174 (drawing) Booth Hansen
pp. 174-177 Lance Gerber
p. 180 (top) Hedrich Blessing
p. 180 (bottom) Booth Hansen
p. 181 (top) Courtesy of Chicago Botanic Garden
p. 181 (bottom) Booth Hansen
p. 182 Booth Hansen
pp. 183-185 Jon Miller
p. 186 Booth Hansen
pp. 187-189 Bruce Van Inwegen
pp. 190, 191 (drawings) Booth Hansen
pp. 191-193 (photos) Nick Merrick
p. 194 Doug Hoerr
p. 195 (top, middle left, middle right, bottom right) Nick Merrick
p. 195 (bottom left) Joe Schmeltzer
pp. 196, 197 Nick Merrick
p. 198 (drawing) Booth Hansen
p. 198 (photo) Troy Walsh
p. 199 Booth Hansen
p. 200 Steve Hall
p. 201 Werner Staub
pp. 202-204 George Lambros
p. 205 (top left, right) Joe Vaughn
p. 205 (bottom) George Lambros
pp. 206, 207 (drawings) Booth Hansen
pp. 207, 209-211 Maxime Brouillet
p. 208 Alessandro Franchini

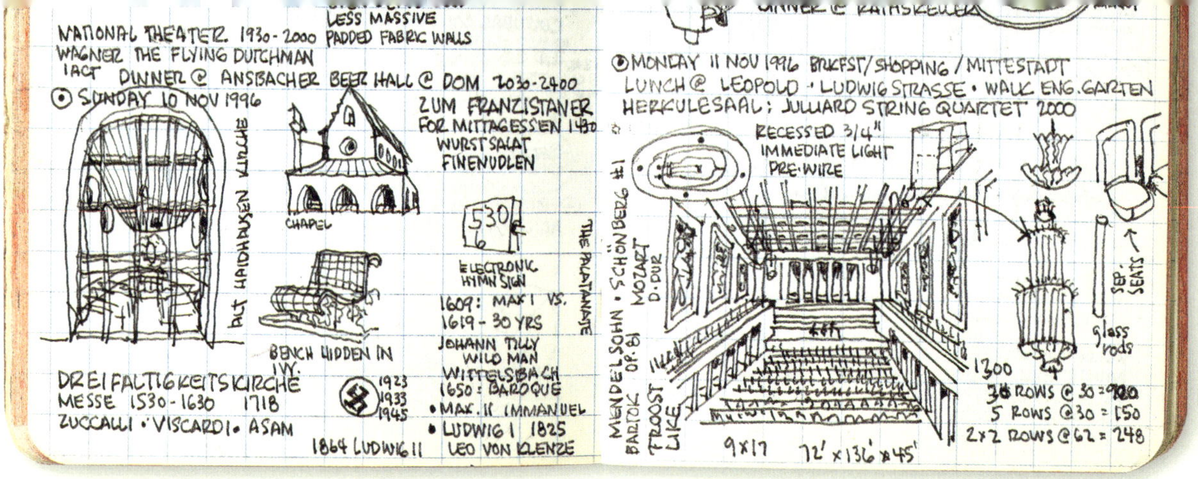
NATIONAL THEATER 1930-2000
LESS MASSIVE
PADDED FABRIC WALLS
WAGNER THE FLYING DUTCHMAN
1ACT DINNER @ ANSBACHER BEER HALL @ DOM 2030-2400
SUNDAY 10 NOV 1996
ZUM FRANZISTANER
FOR MITTAGESSEN 1430
WURSTSALAT
FINENUDLEN
CHAPEL
ALT HAIDHAUSEN KIRCHE
ELECTRONIC HYMN SIGN
BENCH HIDDEN IN IVY
1609: MAX I VS.
1619 - 30 YRS
JOHANN TILLY
WILD MAN
WITTELSBACH
1650: BAROQUE
MAX. II IMMANUEL
LUDWIG I 1825
LEO VON KLENZE
1864 LUDWIG II
DREIFALTIGKEITSKIRCHE
MESSE 1530-1630 1718
ZUCCALLI · VISCARDI · ASAM
1923
1933
1945
MONDAY 11 NOV 1996 BRKFST/SHOPPING / MITTESTADT
LUNCH @ LEOPOLD · LUDWIGSTRASSE · WALK ENG. GARTEN
HERKULESAAL; JULLIARD STRING QUARTET 2000
RECESSED 3/4"
IMMEDIATE LIGHT
PRE-WIRE
MENDELSOHN · SCHÖNBERG #1
MOZART D-DUR
BARTOK OP. 81
FROOST LIKE
SEP. SEATS
glass rods
1300
38 ROWS @ 30 = 920
5 ROWS @ 30 = 150
2 x 2 ROWS @ 62 = 248
9 x 17
72' x 136' x 45'

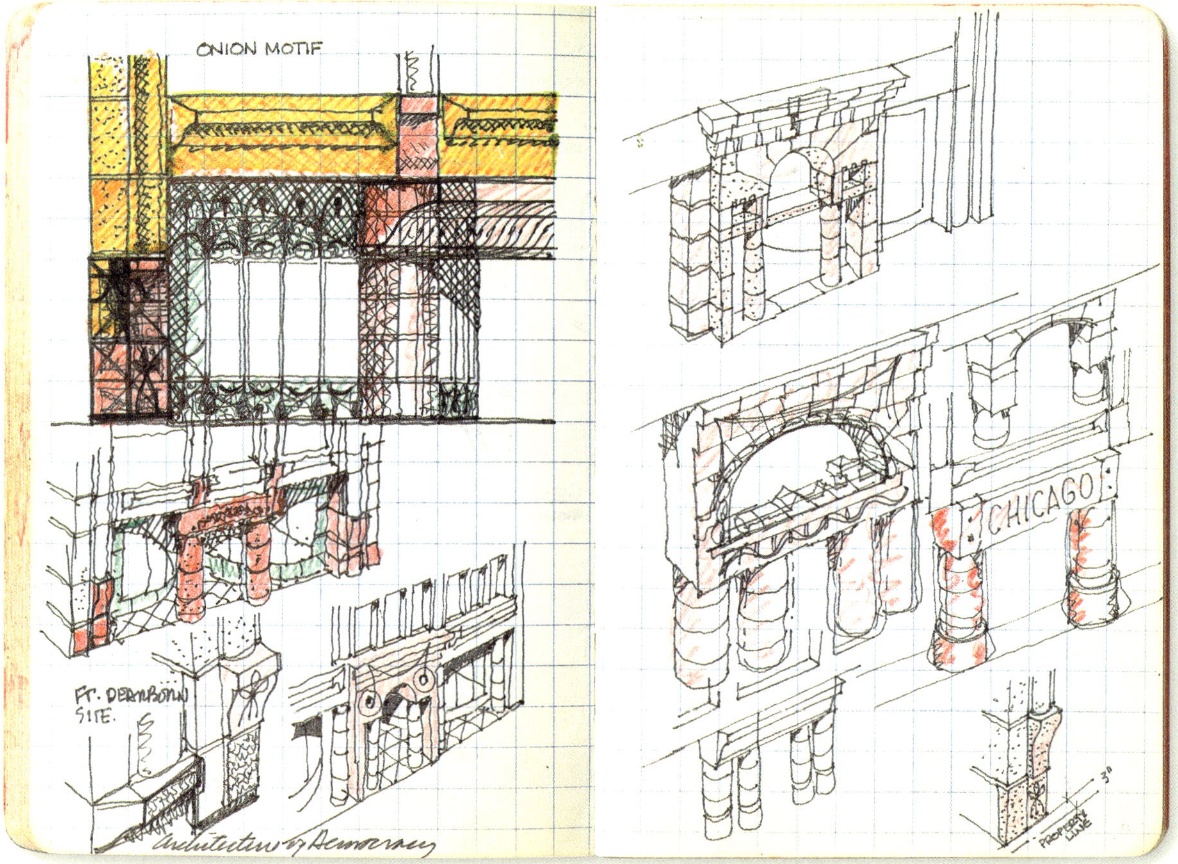
ONION MOTIF
FT. DEARBORN SITE
CHICAGO

ZARSKOJE SELO
Summer Residence of the Russian Czar
"LITTLE HERMITAGE"
GARDEN PAVILLION
@ RASTRELLI
43 PETER I 1682-1725
2 CATHERINE I 1725-1727
3 PETER II 1727-1730
10 ANNA 1730-1740
20 ELIZABETH 1741-1761
35 CATHERINE II 1761-1796
12 COLLEGES TREZZINI
PETER/PAUL TREZZINI
NEVA
MOSCOW
2
0815 BREAKFAST W/ PIANO
0900 BUS TOUR
30% GREEN SPACE
9 MILLION
1147 AD.
RUSSIA 149 M USSR: 290 M
ST BASIL'S 16th c 9 Chapels
VICTORY OVER MONGOLS
IVAN THE TERRIBLE
ANNUNCIATION
ASSUMPTION
LENIN'S TOMB
60'
48'
24'
ФИРМАФ
ВСБАЬЖ
GUMS DEPARTMENT
STATE OWNED

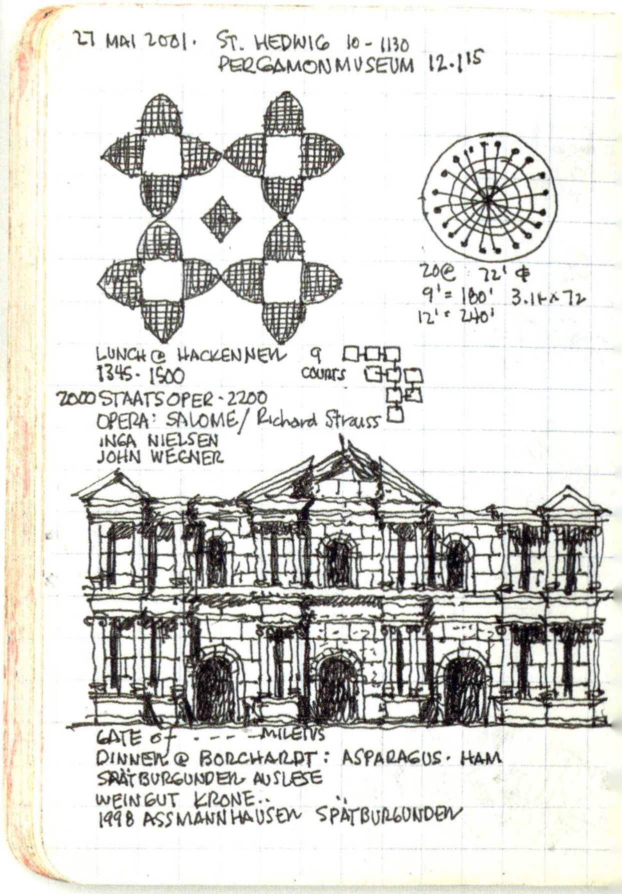
27 MAI 2001. ST. HEDWIG 10 - 1130
PERGAMONMUSEUM 12.15
20 @ 72' ɸ
9' = 180'
12' = 240'
LUNCH @ HACKENNEW 9 COURTS
1345 - 1500
2000 STAATSOPER - 2200
OPERA: SALOME / Richard Strauss
INGA NIELSEN
JOHN WEGNER
DINNER @ BORCHARDT: ASPARAGUS · HAM
SPÄTBURGUNDER AUSLESE
WEINGUT KRONE..
1998 ASSMANNHAUSEN SPÄTBURGUNDER

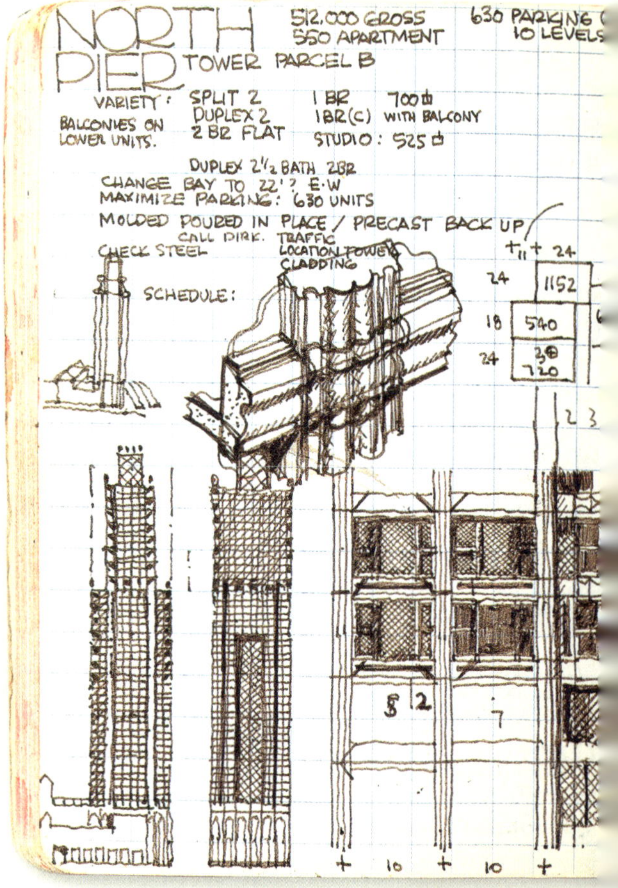
NORTH PIER
512,000 GROSS
550 APARTMENT
630 PARKING
10 LEVELS
TOWER PARCEL B
VARIETY: SPLIT 2
DUPLEX 2
2 BR FLAT
1 BR 700
1 BR (C) WITH BALCONY
STUDIO: 525
BALCONIES ON LOWER UNITS.
DUPLEX 2 1/2 BATH 2BR
CHANGE BAY TO 22'? E-W
MAXIMIZE PARKING: 630 UNITS
MOLDED POURED IN PLACE / PRECAST BACK UP
CHECK STEEL
CALL DIRK. TRAFFIC
LOCATION TOWER
CLADDING
SCHEDULE:
24
1152
18
540
24
10
10